D0949762

INVESTING IN
Rent-to-Own
PROPERTY

INVESTING IN
Rent-to-Own
PROPERTY

A Complete Guide for Canadian Real Estate Investors

Mark Loeffler

John Wiley & Sons Canada, Ltd.

Library and Archives Canada Cataloguing in Publication Data

Loeffler, Mark
    Investing in rent-to-own property : a complete guide for Canadian real estate investors / Mark Loeffler.

Includes index.
ISBN 978-0-470-73759-0

    1. Real estate investment. 2. Renting to own. I. Title.

HD1382.5.L62 2010   332.63'24   C2009-906210-0

The material in this publication is provided for information purposes only. Laws, regulations, and procedures are constantly changing, and the examples given are intended to be general guidelines only. This book is sold with the understanding that neither the author nor the publisher is engaged in rendering professional advice. It is strongly recommended that legal, accounting, tax, financial, insurance, and other advice or assistance be obtained before acting on any information contained in this book. If such advice or other assistance is required, the personal services of a competent professional should be sought.

Production Credits
Cover design: J. Vieira
Interior text design: J. Vieira
Typesetter: Natalia Burobina

John Wiley & Sons Canada, Ltd.
6045 Freemont Blvd.
Mississauga, Ontario
L5R 4J3

1 2 3 4 5 FP 14 13 12 11 10

Table of Contents

Acknowledgements

Writing this book was something I never thought I would do. It just wasn't in the realm of possibilities that I had envisioned for myself. It was a chance workshop, with Philip McKernan, where I announced I was going to write a book, after which I was introduced to Don Loney from Wiley, and he and his colleagues have been incredibly helpful and supportive through this whole ordeal. In addition I would like to thank Don R. Campbell and the team from the Real Estate Investment Network for supporting me over the years and helping me to grow from a beginning investor just getting my feet wet to speaking to large groups of investors and sharing my strategies.

This whole book could not have happened if not for the support and love of my family, especially my wife Mary, who has supported me in every decision I have made, good and bad. To my daughter Eleanor, I hope I can teach you the lessons that have been so expensive for me to learn.

 Introduction

Congratulations for picking up this book! Chances are, if you're reading this you're interested in getting started in real estate investing, or are already an investor who is looking for a new vehicle to help maximize your profits while freeing up your personal time.

Before we start, I would like to encourage you to seek something known as "ILA," or independent legal advice, not just when practising the strategies I put forth in this book, but also when drafting contracts, embarking on new investment strategies, and most definitely before signing anything in relation to deals. Never take what someone else says as fact until you have done your due diligence (which we discuss in Chapter 9). You should always look out for your own interests first and foremost, and take the necessary steps to protect yourself in any real estate dealings.

Speaking of legalities, remember that the documents I have provided are examples only and are presented "as is" without warranty of any kind. Be sure to consult an attorney or other qualified professional to develop documents appropriate to your specific circumstances.

People typically get into real estate investing to experience a sort of freedom. But whether real estate investing is a full-time endeavor or part-time side business, many people quickly realize the investment vehicle meant to provide financial and personal freedom quickly takes over their lives—and not in a good way.

Traditional real estate investing involves either flipping a property or dealing with tenants in some capacity. We will not talk about flipping in this book, so read on presuming my references are to tenant-related investment opportunities.

The most common reasons so many people fail in real estate investing: frustration, exhaustion, and negative cash flow!

Here, I introduce our main character in the book, an ambitious investor, whom we will call Tim. Tim has a full-time job as a banker in the city. For years, Tim looked for something he could do in his spare time that would generate a great side income for him and his family. Family time is very important to Tim, so he decided that whatever investment he made, he wanted to be able to involve his wife so they could work as a team to generate extra cash flow each month.

One day, he speaks with a client who is a real estate investor, has a number of properties and is doing quite well. "If he can do it," Tim thinks, "then I could make a fortune! He's just a regular guy, after all, and I'm a banker! I am great with numbers and can easily line up financing. My wife can even help me pick out our investment property and keep the books!" With just a few hours a month, Tim decides he could generate extra incom—a fortune even, quickly and easily! Why had he not thought of this sooner?

With a song in his heart, Tim convinces his leery wife of the merits of his plan. She reluctantly accompanies him to view some houses, and by the time Tim has found his "dream" investment property, she is even slightly on board —his excitement is contagious! The home inspection reveals a few things that need to be fixed, but nothing Tim can't handle with the help of his brother-in-law, Jack, who is a builder. Jack owes Tim, after all, for helping him move after some failed personal relationships.

Tim arranges financing for and purchases a multi-family duplex in a suburb of the city in which he lives. He, his wife and his brother-in-law Jack fix a few things here and there, and spend three weeks preparing the duplex for two groups of tenants to soon move in. The smell of fresh paint has not even faded before Tim has classified ads in the biggest newspapers in the city, heralding his property for rent. He changes his voicemail message at home to mention the rentals, then sits back and waits for the calls to come flooding in.

Only, the phone doesn't ring as much as he expects, and by the first day of the following month, when he planned to cash his first rent cheques, he has had only one call and no serious applicants. The following week, he decides to change his marketing strategy and pays five websites to post his rental. On three of them, he pays extra to make it a "featured" rental property. "Perhaps," thinks Tim, "people have just missed my ad. It is mixed in with all the rest, after all! If my rental is on the very top of the page, the phone will ring off the hook!"

The calls trickle in, but again Tim doesn't experience the flood he expected. Potential applicants ask Tim outrageous things, such as whether he is willing to negotiate the rent, if he could include utilities and if they could forgo paying first and last months' rent immediately. One odd-sounding woman asks if he will switch the carpet throughout the house to linoleum. "I have a collection of 15 free-range tropical birds, and it's very difficult to clean their droppings out of carpet." Wondering if his ad was mistakenly posted in Lunacy Monthly, Tim collapses on the couch, disheartened.

His wife suggests reducing the rent—the place across the street charges $500 per month less. Tim refuses. They've put so much work into the house that it's worth the money, even though the neighborhood tends to attract those with lower incomes.

More than two months go by since Tim originally purchased the property. The third month is quickly approaching, meaning he and his wife are on the hook for two mortgages once again, since the investment property has yet to earn any rental income. The down payment Tim used for the rental property has drained their savings, and if he doesn't fill the units quickly, he will default on the payments. Finally, he gives in and drops the rent by $200 a month. He then spends the next two weeks filling the two units, just in time to prevent calls from the bank—but not soon enough to avoid some raised blood pressure and stress. At this point, Tim is so panicked, he approves the first two groups of upwardly mobile tenants who come his way. He shoves the keys in their hands and collects their lease agreements as fast as he can, before they change their minds. "Whew!" he says. "That was close, but it will be worth it. It will be smooth sailing from here!"

Fast-forward a few months, and Tim's enthusiasm for real estate investing is a thing of the past. Not only is he still working full time at the bank, his evenings are spent slaving away at his rental property. His tenants, who have bounced all but one rent cheque, call non-stop for all sorts of things—a plugged toilet, leaky taps—and just last week they demanded he change some burnt-out light bulbs! Because the rental contract he pulled off the Internet stated he was responsible for all repairs, he has to comply with their "demands."

Since buying the property, Tim has spent most of his evenings and all of his weekends working on his investment. Instead of spending time with his family as he planned, his weekends are consumed with everything from mowing the lawn to replacing the furnace, from cleaning out the communal washing machine to fixing a flickering kitchen light. His wife has washed her hands of the entire scheme, so when he returns home from the 'burbs on the weekends, exhausted from landscaping and various repairs, he dares not even sigh in complaint. He has heard the words "I told you so" from his wife more times in the past months than he cares to admit.

Tim's situation may seem like a worst-case scenario, but it's not that far-fetched. In fact, it was inspired by true events that investors I know have endured. Every year, more and more aspiring real estate investors skulk away, tail between their legs. They return to their day jobs and bosses, bruised and beaten, while turning their back on their dreams. Going it alone, they become so frustrated and overwhelmed that they completely give up, finding the job they once hated a great relief from catering to their tenants' needs.

"It's a constant race," one investor told me. "There is no more time for me to relax, and going home from my day job each evening has become a source of absolute terror for me. When I get there, my voicemail is full of messages from tenants who want something. I am ashamed to say," she confessed, "that I can't bring myself to check my voicemail anymore."

The best advice I ever received was to find a proven system and follow it. I will never forget an analogy I heard years ago. When walking through a minefield, you can try your luck and traverse the dangerous terrain by yourself, with no idea whether your next step could be your last. But if someone stood at the entrance to the minefield, someone who had made it successfully across not once but a number of times, and had plotted a map to guide you successfully through the field, why would you take even a single step alone? The same holds true for using a proven system in anything you do. All over the world, people spend thousands of dollars each year on diets, following a plan laid out by nutritionists, doctors and, sometimes, sitcom stars from the 70s! Why do anything, especially real estate investing, alone when you can follow the steps of someone who has done it many times before, to the point they have perfected and fine-tuned it to a quantifiable system?

Such a system is what I will outline for you throughout the pages of this book. Follow it, and you will find success. But I warn you—do not detour or dismiss from any part of the system, whether you think it is relevant or not. The principles herein are tried, tested and true. So why venture off the path when a minefield could lie just one misstep away?

HOW TO USE THIS BOOK

In the pages that follow, you will discover the rent-to-own system that I have tweaked and perfected throughout my real estate investing career. I will explain the process, and why rent to own truly is the best investment vehicle for both new and seasoned investors. In low economies, such as the one we were experiencing in mid-2009 as I completed work on the book, rent to own is, in effect, "recession-proof." You will see why, as we go along, that with my rent-to-own system you will receive positive cash flow month after month, regardless of the movements of the markets or the economy.

The material is organized in a step-by-step manner, with checklists or review sections at the end of each chapter for handy quick reference. Also, you will find a section at the back of the book with references and websites to help you get going as quickly and smoothly as possible. By the time you turn that last page, you can confidently begin the process of rent-to-own real estate investing, knowing you are backed by a proven system that was forged not only from my successes, but also from my mistakes.

A small portion of the knowledge I am about to share was discovered as I found success, but the vast majority of it I discovered while scrutinizing my failures. The old adage rings true here, but it is worth the ink to emphasize the point: a smart man learns from his mistakes, but a wise (and, in this case, wealthy) man learns from the mistakes of others. Learn from my mistakes, follow the system to the letter and you will find success with my proven rent-to-own strategy.

PART 1

*GETTING STARTED WITH
RENT TO OWN*

CHAPTER 1

Rent to Own: An Overview

Over the years, rent to own in general has gained something of a bad rap. Typically, these days, the mention of "rent to own" brings to mind bunny-eared televisions, washer and dryer sets and living room furniture procured from a dodgy-looking, wide-windowed shop with signs offering "rent to own" on neon poster board. Only those who cannot afford their furniture would utilize such a scheme, and end up paying an absolute fortune in interest, usually far more than the rented unit is actually worth.

Renting to own a house is much, much different than renting to own a couch. First of all, rent to own in real estate does not cater to those who do not have the money to purchase a home. In fact, the opposite is true! The ideal rent-to-own candidate makes more than enough money to support their own mortgage payments, but cannot obtain a mortgage from the banks because of bruised credit or because the bank wants an exorbitant amount of money down, which they need time to save up. So, what exactly is rent to own in real estate, and what does it entail?

Rent to own (or lease to own—they are the same thing, just using different terminology) is a rental strategy with an option to purchase at the end of a predetermined period. In a rent-to-own scenario, the renter has a reason they're unable to obtain financing at the moment—for example, bad credit or lack of a sufficient down payment. Yet, they want to make the transition to home ownership immediately, usually for personal or emotional reasons. The renters' motivation could be anything from needing a bigger house for their expanding family, to wanting a yard for their dogs, even simply wanting to feel the satisfaction of home ownership and all of the benefits that come with it. Typically, the tenants are looking to stop renting and finally move into a place they can call their own. They don't want to continue bouncing from rental to rental, and are looking to settle down once and for all.

More and more in this economy, we're seeing another type of rent-to-own tenant emerge—the kind who already own their house, but for some reason are about to lose it because of a drop in income. Often, the real reason is more simple: they have over-extended their credit.

Rent to own is a great strategy, when you're helping renters become home owners. It takes on a whole new meaning when you're saving a family from losing their home. Such deals are quick and easy and extremely profitable, not to mention they help everyone involved in a truly powerful way.

Had our friend Tim used a tenant-first rent-to-own scenario right from the start of his real estate investing career, he would have found his experience much different, for reasons you will discover throughout this book. Is it too late for Tim? Not at all. As you will see, Tim is about to have a chance meeting with me, and will turn his strategy around on its head.

WHY LISTEN TO ME?

Okay, fair question—why should you listen to me about rent to own?

I grew up watching my grandfather buy and sell property, and I learned from the things he did. At age 19, I bought my first property, and watched as the deal went south. With one bad deal under my belt, I took a job in sales at Canon, where I earned Top Sales President's Club. I was great at my job, but knew deep down I would never achieve what I wanted in five, 10, even 15 years. I returned to real estate investing, determined to do it right this time. In 2004, I purchased my second property—a duplex in Newmarket, Ont., but I quickly learned that managing multi-family properties was not the best strategy for me. Over the next four years, I purchased more property, but soon after realized that being a landlord was a lot of work! Managing three properties took up all of my time. Even after hiring a property manager, I still struggled to find time to make new acquisitions. Like our friend Tim, I took on everything myself. Exhausted and miserable, I quickly realized that to live my ideal lifestyle, I needed to focus on the things I did well, and create a network of others who could take care of the details, such as maintenance, so I would have more time to spend on the things I value—my family, my career and *my sanity!* There had to be a way to get my investments working for me so I would not have to work so hard on my investments.

HOW A STINKY, DIRTY, DISGUSTING BED MATTRESS CHANGED MY LIFE

When the tenants at my first investment property moved out and left behind the most putrid, disgusting mattress, I knew *there had to be an easier way!* Although I have dabbled in property flips, I knew flipping houses could never be the bread and butter of my investment portfolio. Shortly after, I purchased a rent-to-own property in Orangeville, Ont. This property was just like all the other investment properties in town, with one exception: the other investors were using a rent-to-own strategy and I was not. Consequently, they were receiving fantastic monthly cash flow and a great return on investment, and I was not. It was then that I knew I had to get into rent to own.

I implemented a traditional rent-to-own strategy with some of the properties I had, and found some success. But night after night I still found my blood pressure rising at the thought of purchasing a house on the speculation of a tenant wanting to own that house at the end of a rental period. The stress of trying to find tenants who would love my property enough to eventually own it—before the next mortgage payment was due—was doing my head in. Again, I found myself faced with the same dilemma as before, and again I searched for a better, easier, and less stressful way to invest.

Hour after hour, I would run the scenario over in my head, trying to find the weak part of my investing plan. What was making the process so difficult? Then it hit me: all of my stress was coming from the act of finding the tenant! If only there was a way to purchase the investment property *after* I had the tenant…

At that moment, the proverbial light bulb came on above my head, and an idea was born—one that led to my success and that of many other investors since.

Now, I own more than 50 doors. For the last three years, I have been a full-time real estate investor and was recently dubbed "The Versatile Investor" by *Canadian Real Estate* magazine. Each week, I help thousands of independent investors explore their real estate investing potential through my weekly ezine, *The Secrets of Savvy Investors*. I live in a $1-million house in High Park in Toronto and enjoy beautiful afternoons with my wife and daughter, enjoying the kind of lifestyle and peace of mind a regular day job could never provide.

WHY DO I CHOOSE A RENT-TO-OWN STRATEGY?

Whenever the real estate market takes off, stores are flooded with books, tapes and courses promising to make you rich. During times of economic crisis, investors are shown ways to become rich from investing in foreclosed property. Some find great financial success using these concepts. Most are not so lucky. The difference between these "bandwagon" strategies and rent to own is that rent to own will work in *any* market. As I write this book, times are tough for everyone. An "economic crisis" is in full swing, and people are losing their jobs, homes and financial security. When the market bounces back, the divide between those who survived and those who sank will be enormous. But those who have already implemented a rent-to-own strategy in some capacity are realizing cash flow *despite the market!*

No matter the year or economic situation as you read this, it's a great time to get started in rent to own. This strategy will ensure that, regardless of what happens with the economy in the future, you will thrive.

My mission with this book is to show you a proven way to succeed in real estate investing that will allow you to gain positive monthly cash flow in any market. You will enjoy an appreciation gain at the end of the investment, while having a clearly mapped exit strategy right from the start. These three aspects alone (positive monthly cash flow, appreciation and an exit strategy) will ensure success in real estate investing, and rent to own has them all—and more!

Real estate investing can be intimidating for new and seasoned investors alike. If you're a newcomer, I commit to showing you how to get started in a way that will ensure your success now and in the years to come. If you're a more experienced investor, perhaps with a few properties in your portfolio, I vow to show you a method with which you will maximize profits plus an exit strategy for your properties that are not yielding the desired cash flow. All of this is laid out in a step-by-step plan to help you get started quickly with little or no money (no, really!) with a simple, duplicable process that has been proven not only by me but by thousands of investors across the nation.

There are a number of benefits to rent to own, and we will explore these in the next chapter. However, the advantages of this strategy and the reasons I personally choose rent to own are two separate things.

What I value most in business are integrity investments in which everyone involved benefits. I value time with my family and having a laugh with my friends. Being in charge of my day from start to end is a huge perk: as my own boss, I typically enjoy every moment of my day. Stress is typically a huge factor in a regular job, and simply eliminating the pressure involved with deadlines, co-workers and bosses is worth every mistake I've made along the way. I also avoid any stress involved with tenants, which you will see illustrated in the pages to come. I make my own hours, and never have to put my life on hold (like our poor friend Tim) to run out and deal with tenant issues.

I am no different than you; in fact, if you met me in person you would probably never guess I have achieved such success in real estate investing. I tell you these things not to brag or to toot my own horn, but to encourage you and assure you that because I found success with this system, you can too, regardless of your job title, social status or personality type, your previous investing experience or your IQ.

Seasoned investor switches to tenant-first rent to own, never turns back

Mary had investments all over Ontario. The time commitment was extreme and the return on investment wasn't even that good. One night, after a clump of her hair fell out, she switched to the tenant-first strategy and used the investment vehicle on her existing properties, as well as her new acquisitions. The ease of tenant-first rent to own was enough to sell Mary on the strategy for good. Now, she spends weekends at the cottage, afternoons with her daughter and evenings reading in her large Jacuzzi. Mary vows she will never return to regular investing, that tenant-first rent to own is too easy, and strangely addictive. She has closed eight rent-to-own deals, currently has three on the go, and shows no intention of stopping anytime soon!

CHAPTER 2

Traditional Rental vs. Rent to Own

In a traditional rental scenario, an investor purchases a house and rents it out on a monthly basis, making the transition from investor to landlord. During the rental, the landlord is responsible for repairs. This means that no matter the time of day or how menial the task, the landlord is called out to take care of any problems. Remember our friend Tim, the investor on the verge of losing his mind? His first attempt at a rental investment property had him running to his duplex in the suburbs to fix all sorts of things, everything from plugged toilets to burned-out light bulbs. Tim's situation is a very true reality for many investors-turned-landlords.

In a rent-to-own situation, however, the tenant has agreed to purchase the home at the end of the rental term, and therefore begins the rental process with a different mindset—one of home ownership. Regardless of how great the tenants are in a traditional rental situation, there is always a feeling of lack of responsibility for the property and everything therein. These are not bad people; it is human nature to take better care of something you *own*, something you have worked for and earned, than the care we would extend to the property of another. So, in a rental scenario, the landlord can never feel truly secure that his investment is being properly looked after. In a rent-to-own agreement, since the tenant will ultimately purchase the house, the renter takes responsibility for the repairs and maintenance not just out of a sense of duty; the agreement states they are responsible for maintenance, repairs and upkeep.

Those who have dabbled in rental property before know the true value of such an arrangement—freedom! For readers who have not yet experienced the strain of being a landlord, consider this situation: at one property I own, a home inspection revealed that the roof needed repairs and the furnace had to be replaced. The repairs in total would cost more than $15,000! Who paid for that? Why, the tenants, of course, and without complaint! Why were they so willing to spend $15,000 before they had even purchased the house? Because it's in their best interests to maintain the home and increase their equity while they're renting, since they will eventually purchase the home from me at the end of their rental term.

Speaking of increasing the equity in the home, this is another perk to a rent-to-own system. Not only do the tenants gladly perform repairs and maintenance, they will also upgrade the property and enhance the curb appeal *and* the interior of the house. They take pride in how the house looks, inside and out—*because it will soon be theirs!* Instead of midnight phone calls from tenants complaining that the water heater is broken, imagine having your tenants call you to ask if it's okay to replace the old carpet with hardwood flooring. My tenants have done all of the upgrades on my investment property, everything from replacing floors, renovating kitchens, installing double-paned windows and low-flow toilets—you name it, they've done it. Are these not the types of phone calls you'd like to receive? Any investor would happily answer, "YES!"

BENEFITS TO THIS STRATEGY

As with all investment strategies, rent to own has pros and cons. Unlike other strategies, however, the benefits of rent to own vastly outweigh the risks. We will take a look at the risks in the next chapter, but for now let's explore the benefits. There are four primary benefits to a rent-to-own strategy. First, it's incredibly easy, compared to usual rental properties, and there is far less responsibility for you, as landlord, than traditional renting. Rent to own offers a fixed exit strategy ahead of time, so you know exactly when and how you are going to leave your investment—before you even begin! Finally, the profit and return on investment are far superior to traditional rental property investing, and even trump the returns on most other real estate investments. If you're using joint-venture capital to get started, rent to own is much easier to sell to other prospective investors, meaning you can get started sooner, and partners are far more enthusiastic about opening their wallets. Let's explore each benefit more closely.

BENEFIT: IT'S EASY!

The primary benefit to a rent-to-own investment strategy is ease of management, not just for seasoned investors, but also for those new to real estate. In a traditional rental situation, you, as landlord, are responsible for all maintenance and upkeep. This can encompass a myriad of potential headaches, ranging from middle of the night phone calls about plugged toilets and leaky taps, to other more costly issues such as foundation repair or electrical rewiring. When renting to own your property, the tenant is responsible for the upkeep of the home—after all, it's in their best interests to maintain the property since it will be theirs at the end of the rental period. Rent to own frees you from the responsibility of repairs, maintenance and other time-consuming duties associated with being a landlord. For more on the responsibilities of tenants and landlords, see Chapter 6.

Another terrific benefit of rent to own is that it's an ideal way for new real estate investors to build their portfolio. With a low investment and high return, anyone capable of obtaining financing could invest with rent to own, but even those unable to obtain financing can get involved, as we will explore later when we discuss the different types of rent-to-own strategies and joint-venture partnerships. The guaranteed monthly cash flow will help new investors generate monthly profit and cover costs, while the final buy-out price will enable an investor to build a portfolio faster. Consider yourself warned, though; once you complete your first deal, it can be addictive. Enchanted by the ease, low investment and high return, most investors find themselves itching for the next deal, and most end up holding more than one investment property at a time. Rent to own is an easy enough strategy for even new investors to find success.

Benefit: It's Better than Traditional Renting

To emphasize just how easy the rent-to-own strategy is, let's examine another benefit to investors: the fact that it is virtually hands-off. Once you have purchased the property and the tenant has moved in, your responsibilities are few. It's not an exaggeration to say that at that point, your main responsibilities are cashing the rent cheques and making sure your tenants are repairing their credit. Being a landlord is usually a full-time job, especially if an investor has multiple properties, and it's a job with irregular hours. Landlords need to be available any time, day or night, in case there is a problem. Tenants can call in the middle of the night for anything, and if the problem affects something that is considered a basic human need (such as a water heater or furnace), it's up to the landlord to get it fixed, as well as foot the potentially pricey bill for emergency contractor services. Landlords typically do not take holidays, either, unless there is someone to replace them while they're away. Hiring replacement staff is another cost that eats away at the total return on investment when renting your property. Rent to own, on the other hand, represents a tremendous source of side income, and the time commitment is so minimal that many professionals invest with rent to own while still working full time. The tenant, not the landlord, is responsible for these issues, and that fact alone puts this real estate investment strategy head and shoulders above the rest.

Benefit: No Need for Property Management Companies

Some people choose to forgo the landlord responsibilities and hire a property management company, instead of committing their own time and energy. Although these companies help free up time for the landlord, the fees also eat away at your profit. Property management companies charge you a monthly rate based on either a flat fee or a percentage of the monthly rent. The amounts vary based on the type of dwelling, whether it's furnished and what duties the company will perform. Naturally, most property management companies still charge you even if your rental property is vacant, which means you still have high monthly expenses without cash flow. Avoiding dealing with a property maintenance company will increase your bottom line, and keep your profit as high as possible.

Benefit: Everyone Wins!

In a traditional rental strategy, only the landlord benefits. With rent to own, everyone benefits: it really is a win/win/win situation. Instead of the renters simply paying money each month to the landlord, they build equity in the home as they rent. In addition, the renter has automatic monthly savings (also considered "forced savings") in the form of an option credit. Each month, a percentage of the renter's money is saved for them to go toward their down payment of the home at the end of the rental term. Also, the landlord helps the renters by offering suggestions to repair credit issues, connecting the tenants with a credit repair specialist and reviewing their credit report regularly. After all, it's in everyone's best interests for the renter to purchase the home at the end of the lease term. We will explore credit reports and helping tenants improve credit further in Chapter 10.

It's not only the landlord and tenant who benefit, however. Anyone else you bring into your network also wins—everyone from your realtor to your mortgage broker and even your contractors. But to ensure all parties benefit from your rent-to-own investment, make sure those you involve are the best of the best. We will look closer at forming your network in Chapter 4. You are truly helping people by using this strategy, something that cannot be said for most money-making methods these days.

Benefit: Your Investment Property Is in Good Hands

An ongoing concern for landlords is how much care tenants will extend to the physical state of their property. Typically, a landlord is responsible for duties such as mowing the lawn, shovelling sidewalks and a wide array of repairs. Because the tenant is responsible for all maintenance, you, as a rent-to-own landlord, are no longer responsible for these tasks.

Even the best tenants inflict regular wear and tear on a house, but with rent to own, you are less likely to have a tenant punch a hole in the wall or have an artistic child use the bedroom door as the canvas for their latest masterpiece. With rent to own, simply because the tenants will soon own the home, from day one they exhibit pride of ownership.

Traditionally, landlords need to take a damage deposit when a renter moves in, to cover the costs of repairing any damage to the property. Renters are often unconcerned about the state of a house, simply because it's not their own. They lack that pride that comes with home ownership, and many landlords find that even the most upstanding renters can destroy a house. With rent to own, the tenants maintain the property as though it's already theirs, leaving you with the peace of mind that your investment property is being well looked after. You can learn more about choosing the right tenants in Chapters 5, 6 and 7.

Benefit: Get In, Get Out!

An exit strategy, also known as an exit plan or strategic withdrawal in business, maps the "way out." In real estate investing, specifically, the exit strategy is usually the sale of the property. With rent to own, the exit strategy is clearly defined even before the investment is undertaken. Having a fixed exit plan is a good idea in any investment, but in real estate, an exit strategy is a must! Seeing the end before you begin not only allows you to see the true value of a potential investment, it can also prevent you from entering a deal based on emotion rather than financial return. Rent to own allows you to map out your exit strategy ahead of time, and it's rare when the plan goes awry. The tenant is agreeing to purchase the property at the end of the lease term. The landlord ensures they are able to purchase by helping with credit issues and monthly option credit savings. Barring a worst-case scenario (see Chapter 16), the tenants exercise their option to purchase the home. Because you, the investor, have helped them repair their credit and have given them option credits to help with their down payment, the tenants are usually able to obtain financing by the time the rental period ends—or sooner!

Not only is rent to own a great way to generate income and profit at the end of the term, it can also be used to support any of your investments that are underperforming. I am often asked how an investor can get out from under a low- or no-profit property, and my response is always the same: adopt a rent-to-own strategy! Regardless of how many years of investment experience you have, how many properties you own or how much money you have made in real estate, there will always be mistakes—investments we wish we hadn't made. This can result from purchasing at the wrong time, changes in the neighborhood or emotional investing. Rent to own can turn a bad investment into a good one extremely quickly, and help devise an exit strategy at the same time.

Rent-to-own properties produce positive cash flow in *any market*. This means that no matter what happens with the economy in the years to come, your rent-to-own property will be generating positive cash flow. It's as close to "recession proof" as any investment can get, which means more money and fewer sleepless nights for you.

And of course ...

SHOW ME THE MONEY!

I have saved the best benefit for last—the money! If not for the benefit of profit, we would have no reason to invest. The cash flow and income involved in a rent-to-own investment can vary, but by using the financial analysis spread-sheet featured in Chapter 11 (with a working copy available on my website at www.theversatileinvestor.com), you can easily juggle numbers based on a ten-ant's specific situation to determine the final purchase price and monthly rental amount, as well as your expected annual return!

At the start of a rent-to-own term, the renter gives you a deposit, which you put toward their down payment after the rental term is over. The amount they put forward is up to you, but typically, the amount required is between 2% and 5% of the purchase price. The more the better, I always say, because the client has more "skin in the game." The more the client puts forward in the form of a deposit, the more financially invested they are in the deal. A tenant will have a very hard time walking away from a 5% deposit. The larger the down payment, the less risky the deal will be for you. The down payment I request varies, depending on the neighborhood, town or city. For example, if the house the tenant wishes to purchase is in the middle of nowhere and the tenants default on their payments or choose to walk away, what chance do I have of finding new rent-to-own tenants, or even regular tenants to occupy the premises? Worse, a house in the middle of nowhere will also be more difficult to sell, leaving me without an exit strategy and an investment that will create a negative monthly cash flow. Typically, when searching for rent-to-own tenants, I choose fundamentally strong towns and cities. But if a house is in a remote area and I decide to take on the tenants, their deposit must be high—even up to 10%, to keep my tenants from walking away and leaving me with a property I can't get rid of.

There is another benefit to a tenant to put forward more money, though. Any deposit they give you can go toward financing the property, meaning you will need to make a lower financial investment. If the tenant is paying your entire initial investment, the start-up cost to you is zero and your monthly cash flow is strictly profit.

Rent to own affords a higher monthly cash flow than traditional renting, which is very appealing. As an investor, you can expect to earn between 30%

and 50% per year, but your returns could even be a lot higher. The long-term mean return of real estate is between 3% and 6% per annum. Rent to own generates anywhere from 25% to 60%, depending on the amount of the tenant's deposit, the term and rate of financing, the city in which you invest and other factors (this will be explained in more detail in Chapter 11). Also, the usual expenses, such as property maintenance companies, utilities, landscaping and snow removal necessary with rental property do not apply to rent to own. High cash flow is another reason smart investors flock to this strategy!

As we discussed earlier, the cash really does flow with rent to own in any market. Unlike a regular day job, income from a rent-to-own investment is unaffected by the economic outlook. Traditional renting can suffer in lean times because fewer people are venturing into the rental market, opting instead, for example, to move in with relatives if their situation is dire. Your rent-to-own tenants will not abandon the home so easily. Not only will they remain in place because the house is to be theirs at the end of the rental term, leaving would also mean walking away from their deposit, something the vast majority of renters are unwilling to do. So, while everyone else suffers from a drop in the economy, your monthly cash flow will remain unaffected.

THE MONEY IS GREAT, BUT THE LIFESTYLE IS REALLY THE ULTIMATE BENEFIT

As you are no doubt starting to see, the benefits to an investor are numerous, but ultimately what it comes down to is freedom. A rent-to-own system provides you with freedom unlike any other real estate investing strategy today. Remember our friend Tim, who came home from the suburbs each day exhausted and down-trodden? Tim's situation does not just affect him and his blood pressure, it also affects his family. We have already heard from his wife, who does not keep her feelings secret. Tim is no barrel of laughs himself, and his wife wonders what happened to the man she married, who was fun-loving and optimistic. Tim's children are also feeling the effects of his stress and busy schedule—a burst pipe at the duplex in the suburbs forced Tim to miss his son's baseball game, in which he hit his first home run. As the boy crossed home plate, he looked to the stands, excited to see his father's proud grin, only to find an empty seat next to his mother. Tim's younger daughter misses their nightly story before bed, and she has been waiting for more than two weeks to find out if Harry Potter's wand-up-the-nose maneuver successfully conquers the troll in the girl's washroom at Hogwarts. Even Tim's golden retriever, JT, sits by the door, leash in mouth, awaiting their daily speed walk to Tim Hortons (where Tim always remembers to share his donut with his faithful companion).

Sometimes it's fun to brag about our real estate portfolios (go on, admit it—we are all friends here), but when push comes to shove, what we all want as investors is the *lifestyle*. Traditional rental properties cannot provide this without incurring extra expenses with a property maintenance company. And let's face it, why would you add extra expenses when you don't have to? Tim wanted to live a dream lifestyle with freedom and joy, but instead he is living a nightmare! Rent to own is truly hands-off, and the monthly cash flow allows the investor to enjoy income immediately, as well as at the time of sale. Money for nothing? Well, not exactly, but it's probably the closest you will ever find in real estate investing.

SOUNDS TOO GOOD TO BE TRUE... WHAT'S THE DOWNSIDE?

Yes, there is always a downside, and as a prudent investor, you will want to know the downside up front. But I'm sure you will be relieved to hear that in all of my years of using this strategy of rent to own, I have found only two real down points. They are:

1. **Using this strategy means you will constantly be updating your portfolio.** Tenant-first rent-to-own properties are short-term investments, ideally one or two years and occasionally stretching to three years. You will not hold these properties any longer than four or five years (depending on your generosity, of course) and that means your portfolio will always be changing. Some investors prefer longer term investments in their portfolio, but this rent-to-own strategy will not provide that.

2. **Your rent-to-own monthly cash flow can be taxed as active income.** Your rent-to-own income may be taxed differently than a regular rental property. It may be deemed "active income" instead of a capital gain. When building your network (which we discuss in Chapter 4), find yourself a good

accountant who is also a real estate investor. Your accountant can advise you further on active income versus capital gains, and tell you exactly what to expect come tax time.

OF COURSE, THERE ARE RISKS …

Like any investment, a rent-to-own strategy does have risks, and I would be doing you a disservice if we didn't look at them objectively and in detail. I think you will be pleasantly surprised, though, to see that the risks are minimal and mild compared to other investments. We will discuss what to do if any of these "risky" situations arises (as well as a number of incredibly unlikely situations) in Chapter 16, the one I like to call "Worst-Case Scenario."

The risks involved with rent to own are few:

1. The tenant decides not to purchase the house

2. The tenant does not pay their rent

3. The tenant is unable to buy out at the end of the rental term

We will discuss all these situations later in this book, and you will realize that even these "risks" have potential upsides, making this the closest you will ever find to "risk free" in any kind of investing.

LET'S PAUSE TO CHECK YOUR ETHICS

In any type of business, strategy or even religion, there are always one or two people who ruin it for everyone. Email marketing has spammers. Religions have their fanatics. And in rent to own, there are those who would rather make money by being dishonest than by running their businesses on the up and up. I don't mind coming right out and telling you these people get my goat. Rent-to-own, when done right, is incredibly lucrative. Simply following this system will yield you far more than the average job or investment. This small fortune is gained in an honest way while helping others, and yet there are still some people who would prefer to swindle and lie to people to make their money. *Do not* be one of these people. By maintaining ethics with your rent-to-own investments, not only do you raise the bar for everyone in the industry, but you also increase your reputation in a market that relies heavily on who you know, who knows you and the impression those people have of you. In the years to come as you thrive with your properties, there will be temptation to do things "the other way." In every decision you make, ask yourself if the result will be a win/win for everyone involved. You will find that by helping people, new opportunities will appear and you will ultimately make more money than by taking advantage and doing business without integrity.

ANOTHER WAY TO USE THE TENANT-FIRST RENT-TO-OWN STRATEGY

There is another way to make use of a tenant-first rent-to-own strategy: as an exit strategy for existing negative cash flow properties. By turning a current "bad" investment into a rent-to-own opportunity, you can quickly turn negative cash flow positive almost overnight. Offer existing tenants the opportunity to rent to own the property in which they currently live. This is a great way to get out of a poor investment that is costing you money without having to sell a property at a loss. In fact, you will probably leave the investment with a higher return on investment from monthly cash flow and final buy-out price than you would have received in the first place from your original, under-performing investment strategy.

You can also apply this strategy to real estate investments that are turning a positive cash flow, but perhaps are not giving you as high a return as you would like. At the time of writing, getting a 6% return on investment for a regular rental property is considered a good profit! In rent to own, it's common to yield a 25% to 50% return on investment—numbers that are appealing enough for seasoned investors to halt their current investment strategies and completely switch gears.

IN REVIEW

Rent to own has many benefits, including ease, win/win situations for everyone involved, a predetermined exit strategy and, of course, the money. There are also downsides to tenant-first rent to own, such as having to constantly update your portfolio and having your monthly cash flow taxed differently. Find a good accountant who can advise you properly. Compared to the rewards, the risks of tenant-first rent to own are minimal. This strategy can also be used as an exit strategy for current investments.

Man works 60-plus hours per week, no real estate investing experience, succeeds with tenant-first rent to own, acquires 10 properties in 12 months

Michael, a professional in Toronto, worked full time and then some! Sixty-hour weeks in Corporate Canada left him wanting more, and the life of a real estate investor appealed to him. In an effort to educate himself, Michael spent a small fortune on courses, seminars, webinars and networking events. After trying to get his start in real estate investing all on his own, Michael and I met at a networking event and I told him about the tenant-first rent-to-own strategy. Michael's intense work schedule didn't leave him a lot of time to work on his investments, and he was worried that, despite his desire to begin investing, he wouldn't be able to find the time. This was precisely why tenant-first rent to own was a great fit for him! These days, Michael still works more than 60 hours a week in Corporate Canada, but his little "side investment" has taken on a life of its own. Even without working his rent-to-own investments full time, Michael has 10 properties, grosses more than $20,000 per year in monthly cash flow and nets more than $5,000. How much time does he dedicate to his investments? Maybe one hour per month. Imagine what you could make by committing one hour a day!

CHAPTER 3

Tenant-First Rent to Own: An Overview

A tenant-first rent-to-own system follows a specific structure. By following this, you can rest assured that your rent-to-own endeavor will proceed relatively smoothly. We will look at each step more closely in the pages to come. A typical tenant-first rent to own follows this path:

1. Find and qualify the tenant

As the name "tenant-first" rent to own states, the first thing we are going to do is find a qualified tenant. Finding the tenant is the first step, which is what sets this strategy apart from a typical rent-to-own strategy. There are many places to search for a good tenant, which we will explore further. We will also discuss, in depth, how to qualify a tenant for rent to own based on their current income and credit score.

2. Find the property

The next step is to locate a house which will be your investment property, and ultimately the home the tenant will purchase at the end of the rental term, leaving you with a well-defined exit strategy right from the start!

3. Arrange financing and the home inspection

Unless you're purchasing your investment property right out, you will need to obtain financing for the property for the length of the rental term until the tenant purchases it from you at the end of the rental term. The home inspection should also be arranged during this step.

4. The tenant moves in

After the tenant moves in, you will be a landlord for the length of the rental term. But rest assured, your responsibilities are minimal, which is one of the key benefits to this strategy.

5. The tenant lives in the house for the length of the rental term

During the rental term, the tenant maintains the property and improves their credit, all the while preparing for the day when they obtain their own financing and purchase the property from you. In the interest of ensuring you're able to execute your exit strategy, you will help the tenant improve their credit by offering suggestions, reviewing their credit periodically and directing them toward a credit repair specialist.

6. The rental term comes to an end, and you sell the house to the tenant

At the end of the rental term, the tenant arranges their own financing and you sell them the property. Thanks to your suggestions and their efforts throughout the rental term, they are now "mortgage ready" and will be approved by a lender for traditional financing. At this point your exit strategy comes into play. The tenant exercises their option to purchase, and you sell the home to the tenant.

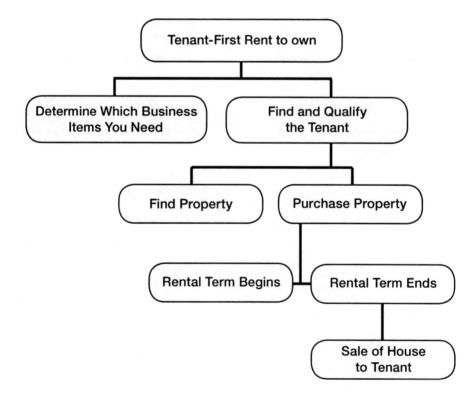

TENANT-FIRST RENT-TO-OWN STRATEGY AT A GLANCE

For your quick reference, here is the tenant-first rent-to-own strategy at a glance.

Getting started with rent to own

Before you begin with tenant-first rent to own or any other real estate investment, I recommend you speak with a mortgage broker who is an expert in real estate investing to see if you qualify for financing, and how much.

One needs relatively little to get started with my tenant-first rent-to-own strategy. In fact, it is inexpensive compared to other real estate investing techniques.

Time

The first thing you will need is time. Committing time to your rent-to-own endeavor is the only way to get started, which means you may need to forgo your tri-weekly hockey schedule or other pursuits. Not to worry, though, it will be well worth it! Your efforts will be focused on posting ads, establishing your network, learning the ins and outs of rent to own, accepting applications, qualifying tenants and, when all is said and done, closing the deal. You may need to spend time looking at properties when your tenants find homes they like, meeting with house inspectors at the time of inspections, arranging appraisals and speaking with the other mortgage professionals you will need to complete the deal. Really, though, compared to the hours of a full-time job, the time you invest in rent to own will be a fraction of a 40-hour work week. This is ideal if you intend to work and invest with rent to own on the side.

Money

Second, there is a cost to doing business with rent to own. But again, compared to other real estate investing techniques, you'll find these start-up costs minimal. Expenses will include advertising for tenants, home inspections and appraisals, closing costs and lawyer's fees. Also, depending on the province in which you're investing, you may need to pay land transfer tax; provinces such as Ontario have LTT, while others, such as Alberta, do not.

Disbursements should also be taken into consideration. When you purchase a house, the solicitor will charge the buyer for any actions they perform that incur a cost, such as land registry fees, title searches, mortgage registration, land transfer tax and title insurance.

At the end of the deal, when the tenant purchases the house, there will also be some costs associated with the sale. Discharging a mortgage usually carries a fee, but you should check with your mortgage professional (which we will discuss in Chapter 4) to determine your final closing costs.

Unless you have a vast amount of money put aside, you will most likely need to obtaining bank financing for the property you buy, which really is a benefit to you in the end. Investing with money that's not your own will allow you greater returns, which we will look at more in Chapter 4. When using bank financing, you will put down approximately 10% to 20% of the purchase price. There are ways to invest without a lot of money, but we will touch only briefly on these strategies in this book, also in Chapter 4. The most common method is through joint ventures with other investors. However, if you're able to get the down payment for your rental property, you will find your expenses to be minimal.

Organization

The third thing you will need to get started is organization. When applications start flooding in, you should rely on systems you have put in place to deal with each tenant. I recommend having a standard information email you can send to potential tenants. This would describe the tenant-first rent-to-own plan and outlines the benefits to them, as well as the things they should be aware of ahead of time, such as deposit, appraisals and home inspections. This way, you can quickly send the information to each interested respondent without having to take the time to write out an individual email to each person. With a pre-written response, all you need to do is insert the interested party's name and change a few details to match their situation, and voila! In less than an hour, you can reply to most of your inquiries without getting a cramp in your fingers or contracting carpal tunnel syndrome.

Along with organization come documents. We will discuss some of what you will need in a later chapter, and I offer some of the forms I use on my website, www.theversatileinvestor.com. Preparing the necessary documents in advance will make sending applications to interested parties quick and easy.

Taking care of business

Another item you may want to prepare ahead of time is a business card. This will be useful if you're speaking to potential tenants in person, and invaluable when networking with other real estate professionals. We will discuss this further in a subsequent chapter.

You should also consider setting up a separate email address to handle inquiries about rent to own. Whenever possible, avoid using the "free" email systems such as Yahoo and Gmail, because an email address like superinvestor354@yahoo.ca can appear unprofessional, and may raise red flags in the eyes of sceptical applicants. If you don't already have an email address on your own domain, getting one is easy and cheap, even if you don't intend to set up a website. Use a domain site such as godaddy.com to find a URL you like. Once you have one, set up a very basic hosting, which can be as cheap as $3.95 per month. The hosting gives you a certain number of email addresses, which you can set up with any email system or access over the Internet via webmail. A client can then email you at info@superinvestor.com instead of a generic free email address, giving you instant credibility.

It's a good idea to find a knowledgeable accountant or bookkeeper before you get started. This person will look after the financial aspects of your real estate investing, leaving you more time to focus on finding a tenant, networking and closing your deal.

Finally, depending on the number of rent-to-own properties in which you plan to invest, you may want to set up a business name or numbered company. A real estate lawyer and an accountant can advise you if this is a step you need to take, depending on your individual situation.

Regardless of whether you end up registering your business, you should definitely set up a bank account specifically for your rent-to-own endeavor. Under no circumstances should you use your personal bank account for things such as holding an initial deposit or taking a down payment. Keep these finances separate, not only for easy reconciliation when the time comes, but also to keep your personal finances straight.

Rent to own is a business like any other, and should be treated as such. You may be investing your own money, but you need to keep the monies from your rent-to-own investment separate from your personal finances. There are small business courses you can take, both online and in person, to learn everything you need to know about the business side of investing.

The will to succeed

Compared to everyday people, investors are a strange bunch. For some reason, we have not been able to settle for the usual nine-to-five, 40-hour work week schedule. We get a kick out of juggling numbers and a thrill out of seeing our projected return on investment. The satisfaction we experience when closing a deal can't be described to someone who is not an investor. And after a deal closes, we look at our bank balances and know that we earned that money not by trading time for dollars from an employer, but by intelligently investing our money. Not everyone can understand this, and therefore real estate investing does not appeal to most people.

Let's be honest, being a real estate investor can be nerve wracking, and it takes a very courageous person to choose this life. There are no guarantees, and most investors make some pretty serious mistakes when they start out. Now, before you close this book and run for the "help wanted" section of the newspaper, consider this: being a real estate investor is something to view with pride. Not everyone is cut out for it, and many people try their hand and quit just as quickly as they started. The final thing you need for this rent-to-own strategy, and indeed any real estate investing endeavor, is the will to succeed. No matter what, do *not* quit, keep going, keep learning, put your pride in your pocket and humble yourself before investors who know more than you. It will be more than worth it in the end, for both your self-satisfaction and your bank balance.

GETTING STARTED ACTION PLAN

The first step in getting started in tenant-first rent to own is to find out, from the aforementioned items, what you're missing and create a plan to fill in the gaps. Use the following checklist and read on for suggestions on ways to get what you may be missing. Refer to the chart on page below for a list of potential things you could do to gather the missing items. Then, fill in your chart and create your action plan!

Sample

Things you need to get started	Things you already have	Check once missing items are obtained
Time (clear schedule, get babysitter, wake up earlier, forgo hockey)	✓	
Money (need approx. $40,000 for $325,000 property		✓
Organization (get accounting system, filing system for office, virtual assistant)		
Business items (have business cards printed)	✓	
Taking care of business (open business back account, take bookkeeping course)		
The will to succeed (buy two investing books, join three networking groups)	✓	

Identify the gaps in your Getting Started chart and cross-reference the items you're lacking with action items on the chart provided. You don't need to use all of these techniques, they're simply ideas for things you can do to close the gaps and get you started faster. Pick the techniques you plan to use, fill them in on your chart and begin using or performing them immediately!

If you took advantage of the powerful tools I supplied, you should now have a very clear idea of what you need to do to get started. Before you go any further, I suggest you take a few minutes to make a list, in order, of your first steps. But studies show only 10% of people who read this will actually do the activity before they finish the book. If you're going to read on without taking the time to complete the charts, don't forget to return to this section later to map out your plan and hit the ground running!

Getting started with tenant-first rent to own is relatively easy, as long as you follow the suggestions outlined in the pages to come. With a little organization, time and money, you will quickly find your rent-to-own deal coming together, so read on to find out how to get started immediately!

REVIEW

To execute this strategy, you must analyze your current situation and fill in the gaps if you're missing some of the things needed to begin. Create a plan of what you need to do, and get started!

**Calgary investor turns negative cash flow to positive
with tenant-first rent-to-own strategy**

Ryan, an investor in Calgary, bought 13 properties at the height of one of the biggest real estate booms in Canadian history. Not surprisingly, Ryan quickly found himself losing money—on all 13 properties at once! He was in the red $4,000 per month, and at his wits' end. At a Real Estate Investment Network event, I met Ryan and told him I could help him turn around his investments and have his property generating positive cash flow within two months. Now, Ryan's monthly cash flow is in the black by $2,000, and he has a pre-defined exit strategy that will have him selling all of his properties to the rent-to-own tenants within three years! Talk about a turnaround!

CHAPTER 4
Building Your Network

There is an old saying in real estate investing: "Your network is your net worth." If you haven't yet heard it, you will shortly, and for good reason. Real estate investing is intricate, and comprises many moving parts. There is no way one person can do it all on their own, which is why you absolutely must establish a good network.

To succeed in anything, especially real estate investing in general and rent to own in particular, you don't need to know everything. The truly smart investor knows that to succeed, you must surround yourself with people who are smarter than you, who have more knowledge of the specifics of the area in which you wish to succeed.

Think of a doctor who goes to medical school for years and first learns all about medicine in general. After obtaining a good knowledge base, the doctor then specializes. Another doctor specializes in another field, as does another. When a patient is wheeled into surgery, these specialized doctors work together to the common end, which is, of course, a successful procedure! The anaesthesiologist doesn't know how to perform surgery, and the heart surgeon most likely doesn't know how to anesthetize a patient. But these specialists work together, relying on each other's expertise to achieve their shared goal.

Of course, as investors, we don't claim to be as well trained and specialized as doctors, but our networks operate in the same manner. The mortgage broker knows his or her role inside and out, as does the realtor. The mortgage broker most likely doesn't know anything about insurance or real estate law, but he doesn't need to; what he does know is the phone number of an insurance broker and a real estate lawyer who *do* know about insurance and real estate law.

This is great news for us investors! There is no need to know every intricate detail about real estate practices, as long as we have a strong network of professionals around us who can advise us when needed and help us complete the steps necessary to close a rent-to-own deal. You don't need to know everything; you just need to know someone to call who will have the information you need when you need it.

It's not enough to be able to say you know a bunch of real estate people. The old adage holds true more than ever in real estate investing: it's not who you know, but who knows you. I warn you, though, establishing a quality network will take some effort on your part. But finding the people you need will be one of the best things you can do to ensure your success, and will most likely be fun at the same time. Meeting other real estate professionals will be an invaluable part of your investing career. They will cheer you on, offer advice and possibly even present new opportunities and ideas that will move you forward in your real estate investing career.

The real trick with networking, which many investors miss, is not just to go out and meet a number of people. Eventually, as you get to know these people, you will end up "fine-tuning" your associations until you have narrowed down your immediate sphere to a handful of people with whom you will primarily work. This doesn't mean you will toss the others aside, of course. But the point here is to identify a "team" of sorts, the members of which will be your primary contacts for the aspects of real estate investing you don't know or are not qualified to complete.

THE NETWORK YOU NEED TO ESTABLISH

You may be wondering what kind of people you should include in your network. We will get into specifics shortly, but overall there are a few things you should look for in a quality associate. First, they must be professional. The guy who gave you advice in the line at Tim Horton's is not the type of person you should count in your network—unless, of course, he's a real estate professional. Advice is free and easy to find, but you need to qualify the person from who is doling it out.

The people you include in your network should be people you genuinely like. The mortgage professionals you will be dealing with will have a huge stake in your success, and the relationship is going to be beneficial for everyone, so ensure that this is someone you truly want to work alongside. If you wouldn't want to sit down with a person for a cup of coffee for an hour, you'll probably run into issues while putting together a deal.

Also, make sure you can work together. It can take time to determine whether you can work with someone, but you will get a feeling about someone right off the bat. Trust that feeling. Some people are not compatible, and some personality types clash—it is normal human nature! Don't force a relationship with someone from your network if it doesn't come naturally—just continue your search.

WHERE TO FIND YOUR NETWORK

Now, you may be thinking, "Okay, these people are out there, somewhere, but how do I find them?" Good news! You don't need some secret pass to get into an underground investors meeting. Investing groups are all over the place, all you have to do is look. Fortunately, for us, we live in a time when any information you could possibly want is only a click away. A trip to Google.com with the keywords "real estate investing network" and the city or town you live in should pull up a number of places and groups you can tap into to expand your investing goals, get educated and, best of all, network.

If you already know people in the real estate investing game, ask them for referrals to quality networking events. If you don't have anyone you can ask, you will probably need to choose events at random, and decide from attending whether the event was worthwhile. Once you attend a few networking events, you will surely find some that are better than others. Watch out for the groups that just want to pitch you their own deals, and have no interest in sharing information and building their own networks, or joining yours. Sample a variety of events to get an idea of what's available. It may take a bit of time to decide which events you should frequent and which ones you should pass up, and that's okay. Eventually, you will know exactly which events are worth your time, and you can attend those exclusively. Larger cities usually have a number of networking events, so pace yourself. Aim to attend one event a week, to avoid burning out and viewing your networking time as a chore.

Chances are, when you perform an Internet search, the first website that will come up is the Real Estate Investment Network, or REIN. This nationwide network is a great resource for networking and building your immediate sphere of people who will ultimately form your "team." For a small membership fee, you can gain access to live workshops, home study programs, reports, books, analysis, seemingly endless forums, investment opportunities and, of course, networking events. Your local chapter will have live events you can attend for the sole purpose of meeting others and establishing your networking sphere. REIN's list of top 10 investment towns for Alberta, British Columbia and Ontario is considered the definitive list of investment areas for serious real estate investors Canada-wide.

REIN is not the only real estate investing site, of course, but it is one of the best. Another great resource is Meetup.com. Chances are, there is already a real estate networking group in your area through Meetup.com, and if not, you can always start one yourself. Meetup.com allows people with common interests to come together to discuss the topic and network. In most cities, just attending local Meetups can keep you pretty busy, and is a great way to get started.

Many real estate investing websites have forums in which people can post conversations and learn from other investors. Forums can be a great resource, but I must warn you that because most forums only require members to verify their email address, there is little or no accountability for the information they post, and most sites have a disclaimer stating they are not responsible for the information within the forums. Therefore, beware of such information and advice, and always double-check the information you receive with a professional you know. You can connect with other investors in forums and never have to leave your house, but I have found that meeting people the good old-fashioned face-to-face way works a lot better, and the level of quality of the other real estate professionals you meet is much higher.

You don't need much to attend a networking event, but you do need to take one very important item: your business card. If you don't already have one with, at the very least, your contact information, you need to get one. Most stationary stores such as Staples can create cards for you in a matter of hours, and a lot of them have online submission services for such basic needs. Of course, later you will want to get your business cards professionally designed and produced, but to get started immediately, all you need is a card with your name, phone number, website (if applicable), email address and perhaps a short one-sentence blurb about your specialty or what you do. For example:

Hypothetical Tim

(123) 456-7890
www.irenthouses.blah
tim@irenthouses.blah

HELPING THE CREDIT-CHALLENGED ACHIEVE HOME OWNERSHIP TODAY!

How to network

For even the most outgoing people, the term "networking" can send a shiver down their spine. For some, the thought of mingling with people they don't know and making general chit chat can cause a stress reaction. For others, networking can cause anxiety simply because they don't like the feeling of bragging about what they're doing, and self-promotion tends to be discouraged these days. If what I have just described rings true with you, rest assured that networking is a skill that must be practised, and it does get easier in time. The right network will allow you to get things done faster, knowing the answers you seek are just a phone call away. Because building a network is so important, let's look at how networking occurs and some of the ways to do it well.

Remember, just as you are attending a networking event to expand your network, so is everyone else. Everyone has the same goal, so set your mind at ease knowing that everyone at the event wants to meet you.

Go with a plan

Before you head out to any networking event, take a half hour to figure out your purpose for going and set a goal. That goal could be to meet a specific mortgage professional or find a mentor. It could be to connect with someone for a joint venture, or to learn about a specific investing technique. Your goal could be to connect with 10 people, or hand out 50 business cards, sell an investment opportunity or get referrals from mortgage professionals for your rent-to-own endeavor. It could be a specific question you need answered. Your goal could be as simple as speaking to one other person—about *anything*. Knowing your purpose ahead of time will help you get the most out of networking, allowing you to meet the types of mortgage professionals you will need in order to succeed with tenant-first rent to own.

Dress appropriately

Sure, strumming a guitar wearing a shirt with giant pink flowers on it, talking about how you can't judge a book by its cover sounds great. But once the smoke from your bong clears, the truth is there staring you in the face: love it or hate it, we are all shallow, and we do judge someone by first impressions. Ripped jeans, long hair and leather inspire images of a biker; black clothes, black lipstick and black fingernails makes one automatically think "goth." This is all before someone even opens their mouths to say hello. Don't believe me? That guitar player with the flowery shirt surrounded by a cloud of smoke—you assumed hippie, right? Caught ya.

Whether you're a biker, hippie or goth in your spare time, when you're at a real estate investing networking event, you should dress the part of a real estate investor. Dress business casual to set others at ease and become more approachable, not to mention appearing professional. Keep yourself well-groomed. That means guys, shave and trim all hair, including nose and ears. Ladies, hair neat! For everyone, brush your teeth and make sure you smell nice! The old adage goes, "You never get a second chance to make a first impression," so keep that in mind and do not sacrifice a professional impression for the sake of making a statement. The only statement you want to make when networking for real estate investing is that you are a serious real estate investor.

Your body does the talking

Just like your physical appearance, your body language can say more to a potential associate than anything you could ever utter. Standing with crossed arms will keep people at bay, hands in your pockets will insinuate you are subdued. Most people have the need to keep their hands doing something at all times or they feel awkward. If this is true in your case, hold something such as a portfolio in your arms. This will prevent you from crossing your arms or shoving your hands in your pockets while still setting you at ease.

Mingle!

Everyone is at a networking event for the same reasons: to shamelessly promote themselves and to meet people who can help them reach their goals. Wait for someone to approach you and chances are you will be waiting a long time. Begin by walking up to a larger group of people and simply listening to the conversation. If you can, join in. Once you have your stride, find the person who has not read this book, who *is* standing by the wall with their arms crossed and throw them a bone. Go and speak with them, and encourage them to talk to others with you. Not only will it make it easier for the wallflower you're rescuing, it will also make the process easier for you because you will be approaching others with a running mate.

When you meet someone for the first time, our default is to ask for the other person's name and shake hands. Moments later, most of us can tell you the precise inflection we used to tell the other person our name and what we do, the strength with which we shook hands and whether we gave the other person our business card with the right or left hand. But we can't, for the life of us, remember the other person's name! Why is that? Chalk it up to pesky human nature again. Regardless of how wonderful a person we may be, we are all vain deep, deep down inside and absolutely love hearing the sound of our own name. Wealthy men donate fortunes to see their names on buildings, where middle-class people donate to causes to get their name in the newspaper. Surely at some point we have all fantasized about seeing our name in lights, have some type of jewellery with our name on it, drive cars with vanity plates and spend hours working on our Facebook profile to get it just right. Our natural default is to listen to our own name rather than the name of the other person.

During an introduction, be conscious in the moment and pay attention to the other person's name. This takes practice. Once you've heard their name, look at the card they give you—really look at it, and pay attention to the colors on the business card. The color and name association will help you remember the person later.

Ask Questions

Have you ever heard the theory that the person in control of a conversation is the one asking the questions? It's true! If you're at a good networking event, a conversation will come to an end and you will leave feeling as though it was the greatest chat you ever had. Then, as you think about it minutes or even hours later, you realize *you* were the one who did all of the talking, and you cannot really say for sure beyond an introductory paragraph what the other person does. You have just encountered a conversation master. The next week you return, determined to find out more about them and have another fantastic conversation, only to realize later that it happened again! There is no magic trick—it's easy to get people to open up when you ask questions, because of human nature—people *love* to talk about themselves! Take control and ask the other person questions. You will know more about them and what they do, and how they can help you in the future. You definitely won't leave wondering what Joe actually does, and how you ended up talking about yourself the entire time!

Follow Up

If it has been a good night, you will leave a networking event with a number of business cards and many great new contacts. Some will stand head and shoulders above the rest as your favorites, while others may fade into memory, to be called upon at a later date. For your new favorites, follow up with them the day after to book a coffee or lunch meeting so you can discuss how you can partner with them for mutual benefit. For the others, a simple email will suffice, saying you enjoyed meeting them and hope that the two of you can work together in the future.

WHO SHOULD BE IN YOUR NETWORK?

Now that we have explored some ways to build your network, let's look at the people you will need to succeed with rent to own.

The Realtor

There are two main reasons you should work with a realtor. First, realtors know the ins and outs of the area in which they work, and can provide valuable insight and knowledge as you prepare a potential deal. If you're planning to invest in multiple markets, you should find a good realtor in each region. Going forward, if you choose to hold more than one rent-to-own investment property, a realtor can bring you qualified tenants who otherwise would not be able to purchase the property they desire. The realtor benefits because they would otherwise make nothing for their time and effort in showing a home; after all, the deals they will bring you probably fell through after a lot of hard work on their part. You benefit because you will spend far less time in the tenant qualification stage of the approval process, since the realtor knows what a qualified tenant looks like from the start.

In a strong buyer's market, the appeal of a rent-to-own program to a realtor is great. After all, if a home doesn't sell, the realtor makes no commission. In addition, the realtor has spent money advertising the home for sale and has spent hours upon hours showing the property. Realtors are under incredible pressure from the seller to get the house sold, and most times a dissatisfied seller will seek a different agent in future. A realtor who can offer their client creative alternatives when a buyer is declined for financing will emerge head and shoulders ahead of their counterparts. In a seller's market, even though houses are selling quickly, there are still deals that fall through and clients who are unable to obtain traditional financing. So regardless of the market conditions at the time you read this, the right realtor will find partnering with you to bring you qualified rent-to-own tenants extremely profitable.

Most investors choose properties near the area they themselves live in, and already have in mind a desired neighborhood where they would like to invest. Rent to own doesn't limit you to just one city or town, so wherever you decide to invest, have a realtor who knows the area well. You will need only one realtor per city, and they can be used over and over as you expand your portfolio in the future. The realtor you choose should not just be familiar with the area; they should know it inside and out! A simple phone call to an ideal realtor should be able to tell you the good and bad areas, the upcoming trends for the city and whether a certain property is in a good neighborhood. They should be able to tell you the amenities nearby, such as schools, shopping centers, parks, hospitals and public transportation.

The ideal realtor is also an expert in real estate investing, and rent to own in particular. As investors, the process for purchasing a property is slightly different than that of a regular buyer. Lenders require certain paperwork and financing conditions, and your realtor should be able to steer you in the right direction with those timelines and documents to ensure the success of your deal. When talking to a realtor for the first time, make sure to ask about his or her experience with investors.

Your dream realtor gets things done in a timely manner. They are organized and forthcoming, which will prevent you from having to chase them for documents or amendments, which will ultimately slow the process and can even prevent a deal from closing on time.

In addition to the resources and networking methods we discussed earlier, another way to find a great realtor is by contacting your local real estate board to find out when they hold events. Attend these events, and make sure you bring your business cards!

Finding the right realtor may take some time, but using the strategies I have outlined should expedite the process so you can complete your rent-to-own deal sooner. On a personal level, your realtor should know and understand your investing goals and be focused on helping you achieve them. Naturally, the deal will be a win-win for both of you, so once again be sure you partner with someone you know, like and trust.

The Mortgage Broker

The purpose of a mortgage broker is to find you the best option on a loan. Just like a travel agent scours the airlines and charter companies to find the best deal on a trip, your mortgage broker accesses dozens of potential lenders to get you the best possible financing. In a time when there are more than 400 mortgage products available to the average home buyer, the murky waters of finding a good mortgage deal can be confusing and frustrating to traverse. Using a mortgage broker gets you highly competitive rates without having to haggle with banks for a good deal. A mortgage broker does this day in and day out, and they are quite good at it. A good mortgage broker will be worth their weight in gold, as with the best possible rate, you make more positive cash flow and ultimately, a higher return on investment.

A mortgage broker doesn't work for a particular bank, so they are unbiased. They will ensure the process of purchasing your investment property goes smoothly. The role of a mortgage broker is to obtain financing and find the proper lender for your investment needs. They know the ins and outs of dealing with banks and other lending institutions for investment purposes. They will not only be able to advise you, they will also be your representative with the banks to get you the financing you need at the best rate. Many mortgage brokers now also specialize in credit repair, and finding one of these brokers will give you a knowledgeable resource for tenant credit repair options.

As with a realtor, finding the right mortgage broker can take some time, but there are some key qualities to look for to make your search go faster.

The ideal mortgage broker is efficient. He or she will waste no time getting on the phone and finding you financing. Paperwork is handled in a timely fashion, and they should be able to advise you of any supporting documents the bank may require ahead of time. This person must be able to arrange financing within deadlines and closing dates and understand that you're not the only person in the equation, that your tenants are also relying on them to get everything done on time so they don't end up without a place to live!

This member of your network absolutely has to be knowledgeable, not only of real estate investing practices, but also of different lenders, their tendencies for approving financing and what they usually look for when underwriting.

Your mortgage broker must be professional. Brokers deal with banks all the time, and reputations, both good and bad, are earned based on their professional conduct. Your ability to obtain financing can be affected by an unprofessional mortgage broker. There are different levels of mortgage broker, and the banks deal with these "levels" or "status" differently. For example, a mortgage broker on a higher level may have their financing decisions made sooner, as well as a number of other perks. Connect with the best, most respected mortgage broker you can to keep your paperwork from slipping to the bottom of the pile.

Just like the realtor, your mortgage broker should understand and possibly even share your investing objectives. Without this connection, you're just another applicant looking for financing. They should have experience in real estate investing—even better if they invest in real estate themselves. The latter is the ideal situation, because someone who invests for a share of their livelihood will take on your investment financing in a way a professional who is inexperienced in real estate investing may not. Again, you should search the previously mentioned resources for the best mortgage broker to suit your needs, and get out and meet with them face to face to ensure you like him or her, respect them and see that they handle themselves in a professional manner. Don't feel shy about interviewing potential mortgage brokers to see if they're what you seek. No matter how much you screen someone initially, though, finding the broker is a process of trial and error, and you may have to work on a few deals with a broker to see if the two of you mesh. It's common to do two or three deals with a broker, only to switch to another broker for future deals.

The Credit Repair Specialist

A credit repair specialist can be in the form of a mortgage broker or a credit repair company. A simple Google search of "Credit repair companies" will yield a number of results, but not all of these firms are created equal. There are techniques that some "specialists" use to repair credit that aren't exactly above-board. There are also companies that offer a "quick-fix credit repair" plan in exchange for a fee, and these are the ones to watch out for. The Canadian government has taken steps to protect consumers from "bad" credit repair schemes. It's actually illegal for credit repair companies to request or accept advance payment for their services. They're also not allowed to guarantee they can fix a consumer's credit without first viewing their credit bureau report. The tenant must receive a contract from the company outlining the process. Ultimately, the choice of credit repair specialist is up to the tenant, but you can help them by including a qualified credit repair specialist in your immediate sphere of associates. Speak with other investors to find a good mortgage broker or credit repair firm they have had success with in the past.

The Real Estate Lawyer

A real estate lawyer is a must in your rent-to-own transactions. Their job is to protect your interests during the purchase and sale transaction. But like anything else, there are good ones and not so good ones. At the time of writing, there are more than 68,000 lawyers in Canada! How does a lowly investor find the real estate lawyer they desire? You could open the phone book and most likely go cross-eyed, or spend days online wading through websites and then begin calling firms in the hopes of stumbling across a real estate lawyer with whom you click. You could also call your local law society and ask for a referral, but you may be charged for such a service, and even then you will not know anything about the lawyer ahead of time. Another idea is to go to www. canlaw.com, a service that's free to you but where lawyers pay to advertise their services to potential clients. A real live person helps connect you with a lawyer specific to your needs.

Of course, the best way to find the real estate lawyer is by networking. Referrals from other real estate investors is the best use of your time, since you are benefiting from the experiences of others. Why go through lawyer after lawyer on your own when you can streamline the process, narrow the odds against you and start with someone highly recommended right off the bat?

Personally, I like to ask a real estate lawyer about their portfolio. What do they, personally, invest in? Are their investments on par with my investment goals? Has the lawyer ever done something similar to what I am undertaking? By partnering with a lawyer who is also a real estate investor, you will benefit from an insight that a non-investor can't offer.

Again, professionalism and a good reputation are musts. They should also be willing to offer you advice and counsel to maximize your investments, and be willing to look over a document on fairly short notice; the ideal real estate investor/lawyer knows that when it comes to turning a profit, time is money!

In addition, the ideal real estate lawyer should have a vested interest in your success. Why? Because they will work harder, longer and smarter if your success means they also succeed.

The Home Inspector

The purpose of a home inspector is to scrutinize a property and report on the condition of a house and all of its systems. It's their job to find components of a house that do not work properly, are beyond their "best before date" so to speak, or are unsafe. The home inspector will also identify areas that may need work in the future, and cite problems from the past that have been resolved. Just like your mechanic's 20-point inspection, a good home inspector will alert you to things you can repair now to prevent serious damage, or to things you will need to fix shortly and a timeline to address them.

Your relationship with your home inspector is very important. Without the thumbs up from this member of your team, no deal can go through. Having a great home inspector on speed dial is vital to your rent-to-own success.

Most people don't consider the home inspector as a vital part of the team— to the investor's detriment. The right inspector will look out for your interests from day one. Cracks in the foundation and other dire situations can be overlooked or go unreported for a number of reasons, but with a home inspector completely on your side, you can be sure that you will know ahead of time of any deficiencies in a property.

Take the time to ask other real estate investors when looking for your home inspector. Ask them who they use and if they find them to be an honest person who keeps their interests in the forefront. As with anything, a home inspection comes at a price. This is one area where you most definitely do not want to skimp. You generally get what you pay for, so spend the extra money and steer clear of those offering home inspections at a lower rate than the average. Chances are, there is a reason for the discount, and when it comes to protecting yourself from a bad investment, the money you spend for a high-quality, reputable home inspector will be worth so much more to you in the end.

Insurance Broker or Agent

Just like the mortgage broker, your insurance agent will scour dozens of insurance companies in order to get you the best rate for your investment property insurance needs. An insurance broker is non-partial and will work on your behalf to get you the best deal. An insurance agent, on the other hand, usually works for just one company and will do their best to get you the best rate within that company.

A good insurance representative is just as important as the other professionals in your network, and just as often overlooked. Many investors, to their detriment, simply take insurance without questioning the clauses within, brushing over the details in the interest of moving on to the next step.

Your insurance agent should be approachable and willing to take the time to answer your questions. You're not taking out a simple policy, after all—you are a business person, and these details need to be explored. The insurance agent should be willing to go through a policy with you, and answer any questions, including whether the policy covers replacement costs (in a fast-moving market, it may not). Also, will the policy pay the rent in the case of an accident, and if so, for how long? What does the liability coverage include?

As with a lawyer, you can always open the phone book or search online for an insurance agent or for quotes. But we are busy investors, and have far more productive things to do with our time. I highly recommend asking other investors for the name of their trusted insurance broker or agent.

Insurance is your safety net, so make sure you take the time to understand your policy and to partner with an agent who is forthcoming and willing to go through everything in detail.

Accountant/Bookkeeper

When embarking on a new investment, many investors initially assume they will keep their own books, but this is not always the best idea unless, of course, you're a CPA or a professional bookkeeper. If accounting is not your day job, however, it is advisable to leave it to the professionals and stick to what you're good at—investing. Keeping your books in order is no small task, and not something to be taken lightly. Letting your books slide or trying to do them on your own may seem like a good way to cut costs and increase your bottom line now, but it will not look so good when you're on the receiving end of an audit. Hire a professional to take one responsibility off your plate and make sure your finances are kept straight—*and done right!*

Chances are, if you're dealing with only one or two properties, you will need a bookkeeper, whereas if your portfolio is more diverse, you'll need an accountant instead. What's the difference? A bookkeeper may or may not have a degree, generally charges less than an accountant and deals with keeping the books of smaller businesses. A bookkeeper tends to be better versed in small business finances. An accountant, on the other hand, will most likely have a degree and can deal with your complex investing finances on a regular basis. Only you can decide whether you need a bookkeeper or an accountant, but partnering with one or the other is extremely important.

As with the others in your expanding network, make sure the accountant or bookkeeper you choose has knowledge of real estate investing. Discuss your plans ahead of time to make sure they understand your ultimate goals. Your financial professional can keep an eye on your finances and perhaps even offer suggestions to keep costs low and your return on investment high.

YOUR REPUTATION

The real estate investing community is very small, and good or bad, word gets around very, very quickly. Your peers can make or break you in real estate investing. The truth is that there is only so far you can go without the help of others in the industry. Which is why, in real estate investing more than any other industry, you *must* protect your reputation. If you don't protect your reputation by insisting on great business practices and integrity all the way, you might as well skip all the networking events and return to your day job.

Protecting your reputation takes on two forms, and both are intertwined so closely that dropping the ball on one creates a snowball-down-the-mountain effect on the other side that gathers speed until your real estate investing career falls off a cliff. The first form is working with integrity, which we have already discussed, but doing business with integrity is so important, it's worth another mention. Don't ever take advantage of someone, don't ever lie and don't ever abuse someone's trust.

The second reason your reputation is so important is because of networking. Remember what I mentioned earlier, that it's not who you know, but who knows you? Well, if 100 people know you and they all hate you, you may as well pack in your financial analysis spreadsheet right now.

If your reputation has taken a hit because you have been working without integrity, your immediate sphere will be affected. When setting up your network or "team," you want the crème de la crème, the best of the best. When the mention of your name sends experienced investors running the other way, the only option you have for your immediate sphere are other dodgy characters. Destroying your reputation in the early days is an incredibly deep hole, and digging yourself out is a lengthy and gruelling process. Protect your reputation by using integrity in your business practices and partnering only with those who are also reputable. Your reputation is your livelihood, your bread and butter, and the only way you will be able to succeed.

JOINT VENTURES

Joint venturing, abbreviated to "JV" and often referred to as "JV-ing," is a strategic alliance between two or more partners joining together to buy an investment property. The amount each investor contributes depends on the amount they have to put in, how much involvement the person wants in a particular deal as well as the return on investment they wish to receive.

Joint ventures are generally formed for one of two reasons, the first being to fund an investment. Especially when you are first starting out, having another investor share the start-up costs can be invaluable, and for some people can be the difference between being able to invest in the first place and having to save for years for an investment property.

The second reason for a joint venture occurs when one investor has more knowledge in a certain area than another, knowledge that is required to complete the deal. This type of joint venture can be very beneficial to both parties, since together they can embark on deals that alone they could not.

When starting out with rent to own, not everyone has the finances to put down enough money to get a mortgage, or perhaps can't get the financing alone because they already have a property for their personal home. When joining with another investor, however, new doors open up, doors to opportunities that would not have otherwise been feasible for an investor on their own. If you're starting out and don't have the capital to buy your first property, or perhaps you're a seasoned investor whose portfolio is pretty much maxed with other investments, then forming a joint venture may be right for you.

For experienced investors reading this book, you probably already understand the concept I'm about to outline, so bear with me. If you're new to investing, or checking it out to see if it's something you would like to do, you may find the idea of buying property to rent to your tenants a bit overwhelming, because the price of houses can be so high.

A joint venture truly allows your returns to be infinite. Many people don't understand what I'm about to outline, which is probably why not everyone is a real estate investor. The misconception is that when one purchases property, they spend the purchase price of the house. Of course, when most people stop to think about it, they know that bank financing means they're not putting forth the entire purchase price up front.

The default way of thinking sounds something like this: "Mark, all of this sounds great, but I don't have $400,000 to buy an investment property for a tenant." That may be true; you probably don't have $400,000 hidden in your mattress. But let's say you start small, with $250,000. "But Mark, I don't ..." Hear me out. You don't need an enormous amount of money to purchase real estate. On a $250,000 property, with 90% financing, you need a $25,000 down payment. If, when you sell the property, you make even $12,500, you have made a 50% return on investment. See, when financing property, because you're not using your own money, your return on investment should be calculated based on the actual amount of money you put down, not how much bank financing you have received. Let's say you and a partner go in together and each con- tribute 50% of the down payment. Now, your investment is $12,500. If you joint-ventured with four people, your initial investment is $6,250. Think you can afford that? Most likely you can, or will be in a position to afford such an investment shortly.

Of course, this is just one example of a joint venture. There are other ways to joint-venture without using a dime of your own money. In this case, your returns really would be infinite, because the only thing you're expending is your time and expertise! Joint venturing is truly a book in itself, so to learn about joint venturing further, visit www.theversatileinvestor.com. Before you embark on setting up a partnership, do a couple of deals on your own. As you do, expand your expertise—learn as much as you possibly can, and turn every conversation you have into a real estate conversation. Learn from other inves- tors and listen to their stories of past investments. Learn from others, but most importantly, *learn from the mistakes of others!* When you are ready, the money will find you. You just have to put yourself out there, and be ready to receive it!

Remember, you don't need to know every little part of real estate investing. Smart investors surround themselves with people who know more than they do. Look for quality professionals and, whenever possible, meet them face to face to establish a good relationship.

IN REVIEW

Expand your sphere of influence by attending live networking events in the area, joining associations and attending events. Find quality associates, including realtors, mortgage brokers, credit repair specialists, real estate lawyers, home inspectors, insurance agents and accountants and/or bookkeepers.

**Investor gets into tenant-first rent to own for the money,
stays for the satisfaction of helping people**

Allison had always wanted to become a real estate investor, but had no idea where to start. After buying beachfront property in Central America and starting a popular vacation spot that not only made her money but also helped out the locals, Allison decided she wanted to invest closer to home. Her first rent-to-own deal turned out to be a "refinance." Her tenants, the Armstrongs, were about to lose their house and had exhausted all other options. In just months, the Armstrongs and their two young children would be out on the street. The deal was good, yielding a solid monthly cash flow and a great return on investment. Most of the applicants Allison considered wanted to purchase their first house or move into their "dream home" and finally feel the satisfaction of being home owners. But when Allison found the Armstrongs, she realized she had an intense desire to help them. Allison's first deal came with the satisfaction of knowing she helped a family who otherwise would have lost everything, and the children would have lost their play room, their local friends, their school and would have had a horrible sense of unrest over losing their house. By working with the Armstrongs, Allison was able to help them lower their monthly payments and clear out most of their debt by using the equity they had already built up in their house. Now halfway through their rental period, the Armstrongs have completely turned their situation around and are on track to be mortgage-ready by the time their rental term is over!

PART 2

FINDING A TENANT

CHAPTER 5

Who Are the Candidates for Rent to Own?

The next logical question is "What kind of person would want to take advantage of a rent-to-own system to purchase a house?"

Potential tenants have one of two problems. The first is that they lack the credit score needed to get a mortgage on their own. The other is that they have the monthly income to support mortgage payments, but don't have the down payment the bank requires to obtain a mortgage. Depending on the situation, the bank can sometimes request upwards of 5%, even 10 or 20%, an amount that most people don't have when they apply for a mortgage. The tenant-first rent-to-own strategy can also help those who do not have the full down payment the bank requires. Let me take a moment to qualify this statement, though. This rent-to-own opportunity is not for people without money—quite the opposite, in fact. As we will discuss further in a later chapter, it is our responsibility to make sure the applicant can afford lease payments so as not to put them in an even worse financial situation than when we started. The potential tenant will need to put down a deposit when beginning the rent-to-own process, anywhere between 2 and 5%, depending on what kind of security you feel you require in order to take on that client. In certain situations, you may need to take up to a 10% deposit, depending on the client's scenario and their location. Therefore, this program is not for people who have no down payment, but can be beneficial to those who just need some extra time to save up enough to appease a lender.

Of course, the strategies listed here help you thrive in any market, but I would like to take a slight detour and look at some of the trends that, at the time of writing, have slowed our economy and led to the dreaded "credit crunch."

Currently, as I write this, it is mid-2009 and the world is in one of the worst financial crises we have seen in decades. America and Britain are hit worst of all, and big companies such as banks and insurance companies, as well as industry cornerstones such as automotive manufacturers, are going belly-up almost daily. Here in Canada, over the past few years we've seen a sharp spike in housing prices. A great example of this was in Calgary, where values spiked exponentially between 2001 and 2007, with selling prices almost doubling. This was due to a number of factors, including a trend in banking that made it easy for anyone, even those with bruised credit, to obtain financing with little or no down payment. People all across North America, as well as Britain, were purchasing houses at sub-prime rates. This trend peaked in 2005–06 and began a chain of events not unlike an avalanche. Even the world's top financial minds could not devise a plan to save the global markets. Those who purchased property during this time did so either at a sub-prime rate or at a lofty rate, under the belief that they would be able to renegotiate for a lower rate when the term came up. In this time, loans and credit cards were also easy to get, and the average family's consumer debt began rising to unprecedented levels.

Meanwhile, riding the coattails of the housing boom, financial agreements that were backed by mortgage payments and housing prices skyrocketed. Between 2006 and 2007, interest rates went on an upswing, and those who bought at sub-prime rates were finding it very difficult to get refinancing. Those who purchased at a higher rate found they were unable to renegotiate the lower rate they had anticipated, and the age of foreclosures began.

I explain all of this to illustrate that even in one of the most abysmal markets we have ever experienced, a rent-to-own system still thrives. Not only does it work in the good times, but also the bad—even in the difficult financial environment in which I have been writing, when banks and insurance companies are going bankrupt, when unemployment in Canada is at 8.6%. To some, this last number may seem low, so let me clarify. In 2005, the unemployment rate was at a 30-year low of 6%. Four short years later, the country is experiencing the highest unemployment rate in 11 years! When foreclosures are a very common reality, a rent-to-own strategy still brings the investor positive monthly cash flow. But I also tell you this because in order to succeed in rent to own, you have to know your tenant.

Meet Jonathan. Jonathan is 32, has a great job on the oil rigs where he makes an excellent wage. Living in Edmonton, he enjoys his job and things are starting to go well for him, but this has not always been the case. Married at 24, Jonathan has recently taken the route of many men before him, realizing too late that he married the wrong person. But his grand realization came at a price. An industrial mechanic by trade at the time, Jonathan had dreams of a white picket fence, behind which two or three kids played with the family dog in the yard. His dreams quickly turned into nightmares when he realized he and his "dream girl" were completely incompatible. On top of everything else, her spending was out of control. On the day he decided to pack it all in, he thought his problems would come to an end. Little did he know that his true nightmares were just beginning.

His wife's spending habits hadn't changed by the time he filed for divorce. By 28, he had a failed marriage under his belt and two enormous credit card balances he couldn't pay. He owed cable, cell phones, electricity, water, gas and heat, not to mention their car payment, three months of rent and 15 store credit cards! And to add insult to injury, divorce is expensive! There was only one thing he could do, he was told: file for bankruptcy. This was not the way Jonathan envisioned his happy ending.

By now, reading this, you're probably depressed, perhaps even empathizing with Jonathan's feelings of defeat and lack of self-worth. Maybe your heart is pounding as you think of his failed love life, ruined credit or limited prospects for the future. But just in the nick of time, Jonathan gets a job on an oil rig making great money. Around this time, he meets Cindy, a 30-year-old flight attendant. Together, they laugh and share many dreams, including the kids/dog/white picket fence scenario. Our friend Jonathan has found his soul mate.

They quickly marry and start a family. With baby number one en route, however, they realize they need more space. But instead of renting, they want a house of their own. They start the search and are shocked to find the home of their dreams at a great price! With an offer in, they find out that Cindy has been the victim of identity theft! Her bad credit, plus Jonathan's bankruptcy, set them back at least two years from buying. The house of their dreams is about to get away.

Jonathan and Cindy are ideal candidates for rent to own. They both make great money and have demonstrable job tenure. They are ready to settle down and genuinely want to improve their situation. Jonathan's bankruptcy has been discharged, meaning they need at least two years to repair his credit. Fortunately, Cindy's identity theft situation can be repaired in slightly less time.

What's next for Jonathan and Cindy? Not to spoil the ending for you, but they will have a chance meeting with our old friend Tim—but not before Tim meets Gary and Rita.

Gary and Rita have been home owners for 12 years. Gary works as a lawyer at a big firm in downtown Toronto, and Rita volunteers her time and energy for various charities. Living in a 2,500-square-foot house in a Toronto suburb, they have two SUVs, a motor boat and a timeshare in Cabo San Lucas. They also live alongside a golf course, where they have lifetime memberships. Both of their children still live at home as they go to university in Toronto, and Gary commutes to work in the city every day. Rita loves to collect antiques, and Gary has a soft spot for Second World War memorabilia. Gary and Rita are doing quite well—or so it seems.

This couple has spent years establishing their status. In their social circles, their worth is determined by possessions, and Gary and Rita have a lot of possessions! To the uninformed, Gary and Rita have it all.

The truth is that Gary and Rita have a lifestyle built on credit. Their vehicles are financed, they have loans, credit cards and lines of credit, and because of Gary's wage, the banks keep extending them financing. Even the Caribbean cruise they took last year was paid for on credit.

It was only a matter of time before things got out of hand. The couple is spread too thin, and Rita feels like a circus performer, trying to juggle their finances each month without "dropping the ball." They have been hit with a disturbing reality recently: sell their house or lose it. Neither option is appealing to them, since they have worked too hard and for too long to lose their family home now. They decide they want to fight for it! But how?

Jonathan and Cindy and Gary and Rita are just two examples of people who would benefit from rent to own—people with all sorts of background situations that resulted in them ending up where they are today. Not only is it important for you to know their situation, you should understand the details, as we now do with these two couples. We will look at that further when we discuss how to qualify tenants in Chapter 8.

Regardless of the market, your tenant is feeling a profound loss of hope. They are in a situation that they can't get out of alone, be it their own fault or someone else's. They have a genuine desire to change their circumstances, and are committed to doing whatever it takes to fix the situation.

Other examples of client scenarios that would fit a rent to own include the following:

Those With No Credit

Having no credit can be worse than having bad credit. To the banks, someone with bad credit can be gauged and classified, and a credit report tells a story about them, be it good, bad or mediocre. When the banks have no history from which to judge a client, they get very jittery.

The good part about a potential tenant with no credit is that they have a clean slate. Unlike with bad credit, someone with no credit may not have the same challenges in changing their ways as they establish good credit. A potential tenant with no credit needs only some direction on how to establish credit and keep it clean. Chances are they will be mortgage-ready in a shorter period of time, and their rent-to-own term will be less than that of someone with bad credit.

Those with no credit are often younger, as many young people these days are choosing to stay away from credit in order to prevent a bad credit situation in the future. Their intentions are good, but they find out even though they have avoided a bad credit situation, they are still no better off.

Those New To the Country

When you immigrate, your credit from your original country doesn't follow you—consider it confiscated at customs. Newcomers are in the same boat as those without credit. They need time to prove their worth to a bank before they can get mortgage financing.

Regardless of their credit and payment history in their home country, those who immigrate find it very difficult to get any credit immediately. Even things such as cell phone accounts and utility companies will assess this client a deposit, which is held for a predetermined period, solely because the company has no idea what their payment history is like. Before the credit crunch, it was easier for people new to the country to obtain financing, but since the banks have cracked down on lending to those with anything less than good credit, immigrants are unable to purchase a house right away when they arrive, despite their financial circumstances.

These types of people can be your best tenants. Chances are, they had great credit back home and their payment habits are sound. After a harrowing immigration process, most people who are new to the country are eager to get settled in and finally have the process over once and for all. To bounce from apartment to apartment after all the work they did to get here is an exhausting prospect, and immediately moving into the house they will eventually own is extremely appealing.

A tenant I dealt with in the past had just moved to Canada from Australia. He was in a very well-paying line of work, but didn't have the job tenure or Canadian credit to obtain financing. With a few pointers on ways to establish good credit, he was able to exercise his option to purchase within two years.

People Who Have Been Through Bankruptcy

Bankruptcy does a number on a person's credit, and most lenders need to see at least two years of good payment history on a person's bureau report after discharge before they will consider them for a mortgage. This is also the time it usually takes for someone to repair their credit enough to be considered for a mortgage.

More and more, you will see people with high incomes declaring personal bankruptcy. It's a legal process that allows the debtor relief from their situation, as no creditor who is unsecured can initiate collection proceedings or garnish wages during this time. Often, people are advised to declare bankruptcy too soon, and the process is gaining popularity as a "way out" and a "fresh start." Unfortunately, bankruptcy has a huge impact on an individual's ability to qualify for a mortgage, and it takes approximately two years to repair one's credit after the date of discharge.

Medical issues are one of the main reasons people find they have to declare bankruptcy. Even though in Canada our medical expenses are mostly covered by the government, some illnesses require extra payments for treatment and medication that the average person can't afford. Making these payments for treatment to save one's life becomes the priority (and rightfully so), and the regular bill payments and repaying debtors tends to fall by the wayside. Most times, the illness will also keep a person off work, so as their expenses go up, their income falls off completely so even having extended health insurance is not enough to keep the proverbial wolves at bay.

Once the medical condition is resolved and the patient is back on their feet, they face the massive task of also recovering financially. Even though their income returned, they are still saddled with the bankruptcy on their credit file, and another two years following their discharge date to even be able to be considered for a mortgage.

Divorce is another major reason for declaring bankruptcy. In fact, one-third of all bankruptcies are caused by separation or divorce. This occurs because as one's income stays the same, suddenly their expenses double, as they are no longer splitting the payments for things such as housing, utilities and debt repayment with a spouse. Divorcees find it difficult to continue repaying their debts at the same time as keeping on top of the bills, and if one party is assigned to pay child support or alimony, bankruptcy can seem to be the only option. Often, the divorcee soon has their finances back in order and is ready to start fresh, perhaps with a new "someone special," but they are unable to buy a house to complete their ideal new life because the bankruptcy is not yet discharged, or there hasn't been enough time to clean up the credit. It can be incredibly frustrating—as Tim's applicant Jonathan discovered.

One of the most common reasons for bankruptcy in this economy is job loss. With so many jobs disappearing, and many more at risk, if a family has not experienced layoffs due to the economic crisis, they know someone who has been let go. These people usually were high up on the company totem pole and were originally making quite good money in their position. Those with higher incomes tend to have the lifestyle (and subsequent debt) to match, and once the well-paying job is gone, they are no longer able to service the debts while still paying their bills. For some, bankruptcy can be the only option after a job loss. It's only a matter of time until the individual finds a new job, but it is often too late to save their situation.

Those who have been through a bankruptcy believe they can't even consider getting a home until their bankruptcy is discharged. You may only encounter those who are still in bankruptcy every now and again, since most people know they will need time to repair their credit.

Those With Past Health Issues

When someone is seriously ill and facing medical bills that go over and above public health care, the last thing on their minds is maintaining their credit score. Often, they have no other choice but to let their other payments slide in the interest of staying alive.

Health issues do not always equal bankruptcy. A recovering patient may have only very badly bruised credit, in which case they are ideal for rent to own. A debt repayment plan and implementing other credit repair techniques (which we will discuss when we look at ways to help a tenant repair their credit) could be all they need to clear up their situation and be mortgage-ready.

Small Business Owners

Most times, small business owners get the raw end of the stick when it comes to mortgage financing. Although there are some companies that have special programs aimed at small business owners, such borrowers generally need to display two years of business history to be considered.

Lenders can sometimes work off declared income, but they usually need to see two years of business activity. Any business owner can tell you that it takes a few years to get established, and even if they have been profitable for a few years, it may not be enough to get a mortgage.

Those Who Are Divorced

As Jonathan discovered, divorce can do a number on your credit. Many divorcees take advantage of a rent-to-own program as they establish themselves alone and get back on their feet.

Bankruptcy is an extreme solution to credit issues created by divorce. Sometimes the divorcee's credit is merely bruised, not leaving them in complete financial ruin but inflicting enough damage to prevent them from starting their romantic new independent life.

Victims of Identity Theft

In this day and age, with ATM skimming, phishing, spam and a whole lot of other jargon that didn't even exist a decade ago, more and more people are finding out that "they" have been on spending sprees—and have nothing to show for it! Getting the problem straightened out does not happen overnight. In fact, it's quite a long process filled with investigations, and even after all of that, the victim's credit can still be damaged.

These people have been victimized by diabolical criminals, and are usually targeted for a reason, such as having a lot of credit or can obtain a lot of credit. You won't hear many stories about a person with bad credit becoming the victim of identity theft. Without doing anything wrong, their lives are completely disturbed and their dreams of home ownership shattered. If they have good payment history to start, with a little direction a victim of identity theft can clean up their credit within a few years. These people usually make excellent tenants, as they are already responsible and are eager to rectify matters so they can get on with their lives.

Those Who Were Just Plain Dumb In The Past

"I was young and stupid" is the mantra of this group, but they have changed their ways and are eager to prove it to anyone who gives them the chance. Make sure when dealing with these people that their mantra includes "in the past" and they are genuinely dedicated to changing their ways.

Proceed with caution with these people, and trust your instincts. Many people genuinely do just need a second chance, and if they have genuinely changed their ways they will be eager to begin a credit repair program and incredibly thankful to you for giving them the opportunity to own a home.

This is just a snapshot of the types of people who would find a tenant-first rent-to-own program. There may be other situations you will come across that could fit in, so don't limit your tenants to the above scenarios, but do make sure you ask the appropriate questions. We will talk about some of these "appropriate" questions when we learn to qualify a tenant in an upcoming chapter. Now that you have an idea about your ideal rent-to-own tenant, let's look at how to find these people!

IN REVIEW

When searching for your tenant, look for those with no credit, those new to the country, people who have been through bankruptcy, those with past health issues, small business owners, divorcees and victims of identity theft.

Tenants with low deposit get rent-to-own house within six months!

Grayson and Holly applied for tenant-first rent to own in the early months of 2008, but didn't qualify, as they had only $2,000 to put down and they required a minimum of $8,000. They were motivated, though, aware that rent to own was the best option for them to get a house despite their current credit issues. They asked for a payment plan for the deposit, and I agreed to take $500 per month from them and put it in trust with a lawyer until they had the full $8,000 and could take advantage of the program. Originally, we talked about their payment plan lasting 12 months. But to my surprise and delight, Grayson and Holly had the full deposit needed within six months! With the full amount in trust, we started their house hunt and shortly after they found the home of their dreams! At the time of writing, Grayson and Holly have been working hard to repair their credit and are in great shape to be able to purchase the house at the end of their rental term, which will be up in just eight months. They are excited to finally own their own home, and could not have done it without the payment plan we set out for them.

CHAPTER 6

The Secret Is the Tenant-First Strategy

A traditional rent to own looks something like this: the investor purchases a property and then searches for a tenant. A rental term is agreed upon based on how much time the client will need to become mortgage-ready, and monthly rent and a final purchase price are determined. The tenant moves in and the rent to own begins.

Let's check in with our friend Tim. He has tenants renting his property, and they were the best he could get in the time he had before the bank demanded their next mortgage payment. Having threatened two of his tenants with eviction just two weeks earlier, Tim was ready to start again with new, reliable tenants (ones who actually pay their rent!), but was nervous that he was just going to get into the same cycle with new tenants. With his wife on his case, Tim knew he had to change something or be sleeping on the couch for years to come! The crick in his back was enough to motivate him to plug into a network of other real estate investors. Exhausted with his rental property and nearing the end of his rapidly fraying rope, Tim stumbled into a weekly real estate investing group meeting, where he connected with an investor who suggested he use a rent-to-own strategy with his existing property. Not only would he be off the hook for maintenance and recover his valuable family time, he would also have a solid exit strategy for the end of the rental term that would yield him enough profit to begin expanding his real estate portfolio.

Tim arrived home that night on a high, and was excited to tell his wife about the strategy. He was disillusioned, though, when she didn't share his excitement. "It sounds to me like it will be even harder to find someone who wants to purchase the house than it is to find a reliable tenant!" A bit deflated, Tim read his wife's expression and dutifully picked up his pillow and returned to the couch, where he tossed and turned all night, trying to think of a better solution.

Most investors embarking on a rent-to-own strategy begin this way—even I did at the start of my real estate investing career. Both in theory and on paper, a traditional rent to own seems like a good plan. For certain investors, the traditional rent-to-own strategy works well, and the benefits are similar to the strategy you have been learning—return on investment is strong, the investor receives monthly cash flow, the tenant is responsible for maintenance and repairs and the exit strategy is defined at the outset. But there is one variable to the traditional rent-to-own strategy that can make it incredibly frustrating—*finding a tenant!*

When an investor purchases a property and then searches for someone who will ultimately love the house enough to purchase it in the end, it's quite a gamble. The amount of work that goes into finding the perfect tenant can be great and the process lengthy. Plus, what if they never find that perfect person?

I was having a sleepless night similar to Tim's (minus the couch and the back pain, of course!) when I formed my tenant-first strategy. I lay there, thinking about how great rent to own would be if qualified, motivated tenants would come to me, with house and all, ready to go. That's when it hit me: why couldn't the tenants simply come to me? Suddenly, everything began falling into place.

THE TENANT-FIRST STRATEGY

My tenant-first strategy is simple; the tenant selects their own house to rent to own. Not only are they emotionally invested in the property because they have chosen it, you also know right off the bat that you have reliable and loyal tenants who will maintain the house and keep their payments coming without fail, because you're giving them the opportunity to own their dream house. Also, with the tenant in place, there is no need to worry about the property being unoccupied, leaving you with no monthly cash flow. By finding the tenant before the property, you save yourself a lot of unnecessary stress and hassle!

Lucky for Tim, the night after his horrible sleep on the couch, he attended a networking event, where he learned of the tenant-first rent-to-own program. He knew immediately that he had to switch gears and begin again, this time with a proven, step-by-step plan to generate the monthly cash flow and return on the investment he wants. Again, Tim returns home to his wife and tells her of a new strategy, one that could prove incredibly profitable while at the same time allowing him the time with his family he so values. It takes Tim more than an hour to convince his wife to listen to him, but once her attention is completely his, she sees how the strategy can be exactly what they are looking for. To that point, Tim's investment property was driving him insane, leaving him exhausted and in the dog house. But by changing a few things, he could start over with fresh tenants and new property, and best of all, a clean slate.

It takes Tim and his wife (who is once again fully on board, thank goodness!) a few months to evict their slack-jawed tenants for non-payment. During this process, Tim puts the word out to find a rent-to-own tenant for this property, one who will be responsible for all of the maintenance and upkeep, not to mention actually making their monthly rent payments. Using rent to own as an exit strategy for his under-performing investment property is about to prove one of the best decisions Tim has ever made.

At another real estate investment networking event, Tim finds another investor looking to joint-venture and speaks with him about the tenant-first rent-to-own strategy. He is, after all, almost maxed out on the credit he can get from a bank. With an investing partner, however, he could be approved for another property—this time using the tenant-first strategy. Let's now follow Tim as he searches once again for tenants, but this time, they are rent-to-own tenants who will choose their house after being approved.

WHERE TO FIND TENANTS

There are a number of ways to find tenants, but my favorite methods are the low-cost ones. The less you can spend on marketing, the better your bottom line. You can place ads in a variety of outlets, but by far the best media for this is online. House hunters and renters alike swarm the Internet in their housing search, where they are able to look at pictures of potential properties and view prices, all from the comfort of their PC. Reaching out to these people via the web is by far the best use of your time and money. You get far more bang for your buck, and you can write descriptions and post pictures. By focusing locally in a particular area, you will receive a more targeted base of inquiries, preventing you from wasting time with people who are not educated about the area in which you wish to invest. The Internet also allows you to reach more qualified people than traditional means of advertising. For more precise results, search for rental forums and online bulletin boards in your city or town, but here are a few nation-wide resources to get you started.

Online classifieds

Craigslist.com and Kijiji.com are two excellent examples of online classifieds websites, and although they are arguably the two biggest players, they're not the only two sites on which one can advertise a rent to own. Search local sites that are specific to the town or city in which you are investing. For example, type "find rental property in Calgary" or "apartment finder Winnipeg." Chances are you will find a number of other worthwhile websites that target house hunters locally.

There are two ways to use online classifieds to spread the word about your rent-to-own opportunity:

1. Post to advertise the opportunity

In the "housing wanted" section (or something similar), post an ad telling people about rent to own. This ad will not only serve you now, as potential tenants can view it and respond, it will also do well in the future. Most things that are posted online stay there indefinitely, or at least for many months before old records are purged. Your ad will serve as an advertising piece when people search the terms in your ad, and your post shows up in their search results. Here is an example of a good post for a web classified:

> *Do you have good income but bad credit? Looking to take a step toward home ownership? We can help! Choose your house and rent to own with 20% of your rent going toward your down payment! Contact for more details (123) 456-7890 or email soandso@awesomewebhosting.com*

Here's another example:

> *Rent to own the house of your choice!*
> *If you have good income but bruised credit, home ownership is within your reach. Stop wasting money on rent and start building equity in your own home today! Call (123)456-7890 for more information on how you can take the first step toward home ownership, despite your credit!*

2. Respond to ads already posted by those looking for housing

You can also reply to ads others have posted stating they are looking to rent an apartment or a house. Often you will also see ads posted by people looking to do a rent to own! A typical ad will look something like this:

House wanted to rent for July 1st for a growing family. Husband, wife, one-year-old baby and another on the way. Must be pet friendly, as we have a very well-trained, well-behaved dog. Must have a yard. Looking in the Richville area of the city. References available.

This is a great ad to reply to, for a number of reasons. They are a growing family, and are obviously looking for a bigger place, and to upgrade from an apartment to a house. This is the first step toward home ownership, so a rent to own would appeal to them because they can make the transition to home ownership immediately and save the hassle and stress of having to move again in a few months or years. Clearly, there is a reason they have not decided to buy, and it is a pretty safe assumption that this reason involves poor credit.

When responding to ads on web classifieds, watch out for a few phrases that should prove a big flashing neon sign that they are not the tenants you seek. For example:

Single mother of four looking to rent house, need more room. Can spend no more than $900 per month. Would like to have utilities included.

This ad would repel me for a number of reasons. First, a single mother will not have as much disposable income as a married couple, simply because there is only one person able to gain income rather than two. Second, the fact that she has four kids means there is probably a strain on her finances as it is. Third, she has designated the amount she would like to spend is $900. This is too low for the average lease payment, and that shows me she probably cannot afford a rent to own. Lastly, the request to have utilities included in her payment shows that she would like to streamline things for less responsibility, and therefore is probably not ready to make the transition to home ownership.

A few years ago, it seemed as though every book, television program and newspaper advice article was heralding the benefits to home ownership. "Why not buy instead of rent?" they asked. "After all, renting is like flushing your money down the toilet! Everyone who can buy a house should, as soon as possible, and begin building equity instead of 'flushing' it for even another day in a rental situation!" And so, renters young and old, rich and poor ran to the bank to try to get out of their "bad" rental situation and into their own home.

While it's true that a mortgage payment is a better use of your money than paying to rent a house each month, home ownership is not for everyone at every stage in life. Owning a home is a big responsibility. Maintenance, upkeep, yard work, property tax, closing costs, condo fees and other factors often shock new home owners, and they find they're not ready to keep up with the added responsibility and stress that comes with owning a home. The truth is, renting is not such an evil thing! For some people, a rental situation is actually better for them if they are unwilling or unable to care for the property or don't have the life experience to pay bills and deal with any problems that may arise. In the last year or two, there has been a shift in thinking, and more and more people are saying that home ownership, though rich in benefits, is not a decision to be taken lightly or rushed into. The buyer has to be *ready* for the responsibility of a home, and some people just are not at that point in their lives. *There is nothing wrong with renting.* For some, it's the wise decision. Besides, without renters, real estate investors would have no tenants.

This is clearly the case with the woman who posted the above ad in a web classified forum. In just three sentences, I could tell she is not the type I am looking for, and if you keep in mind the responsibility factor of home ownership, you will be able to quickly spot, and dismiss, those who should continue renting for now.

When responding to an ad on a web classifieds site, I keep it short and sweet; after all, I am only checking interest. If they reply, I can give them more information, but initially I only want to pique their interest and prompt them to initiate contact with me. My reply to their post for housing wanted will read something like this:

> Hi there, (name, if it's included in their post)
> I saw your posting for a house to rent on awesomewebclassifieds.com, and just wanted to send you a quick email to ask if you have ever thought about renting to own instead of just plain renting? I have a program where you choose your own house, and 20% of your monthly lease payment is held for

you in an option credit to go toward your down payment at the end when you purchase the house. If you'd like more information, please email me at myname@mynsme.com, or give me a call at (123) 456-7890.
I'm looking forward to discussing the program with you!

I sign it with my name and contact information, and then I wait to see if the person replies. When they do, I explain the rent-to-own program in detail either over the phone or via email or direct them to my website for more information. A website can serve you well in this situation, preventing you from spending hours on the phone telling potential applicants the same things over and over, but make sure you follow up with the applicant to see if they have any questions. When directed to a website, the majority of people will not follow through unless directly prompted. It would be a shame to lose a quality applicant, so make sure you give them a quick call or send them an email as a follow-up action.

Online housing locator websites

Another place to post ads and reply to housing wanted ads is on housing locator websites such as viewit.ca, rentfaster.ca and places4rent.com. These sites are usually not free to post, but the appeal is that they are free for house hunters to use, and therefore attract a lot of traffic. You can post a blurb with similar word count as newspaper classifieds, and you can also post a photo if you choose. Be sure you don't mislead: since you don't already have a property to advertise, if you post a picture of a gigantic house, make sure that your text explains that clients can choose their own house so they don't assume they are applying for the one in the photo.

The advertising text for a housing locator website is much the same as what we used for online classifieds sites. It's a good idea to write more than just a brief blurb, though, since those who use these sites are looking for as much detail as possible to quickly and efficiently narrow their search. People who use these websites don't want to spend all day scrolling through hundreds and hundreds of classified ads. Because of their search refinement tools, these types of housing locator sites appeal to house hunters who are in a hurry or get irritated with a lot of unnecessary steps. Give these people a little more to consider, for example:

Why rent when you can buy?

If the only thing standing between you and the house of your dreams is bruised credit or a small down payment, we may be able to help you achieve your goals of home ownership. You select the house you want to rent to own, so moving into the house of your dreams is finally within reach! Don't spend another month making your landlord rich. Apply your monthly rent payments toward a rent to own, and build equity in the house of your choice while you repair your credit. Own your dream home in one to three years!

Post ads in the newspaper

There are two types of newspapers I use. One is the free local commuter news-papers, such as *Metro*. These papers don't cost the reader anything, and are a great way to get your message out there. You can also post an ad in a local com-munity newspaper, which may not have quite as large a circulation, but is also a great resource. The cost to place a classified ad is minimal, but you definitely don't get quite the same bang for your buck as when you post online. A classi-fied ad in a print newspaper can cost anywhere from $50 to $185 for the first week, but most papers will give a discount of up to 50% for each week after the first. The good news about posting a classified ad with a newspaper these days is that most newspapers, both free and paid, also have their classified ads on-line, essentially tripling their readership! Moreover, the newspaper will usually add on the posting online for about $10. Is that worth it? You bet it is!

When posting an ad in the classified section of your local newspaper, you are restricted with your wording. You'll need to make your ad powerful enough to capture the attention of a potential tenant with a very small number of words, while at the same time compelling them to want more information. Classified ads for newspapers and their websites need to say as much as possible in the short headline to catch the reader's attention and encourage them to read on. This can be tricky, but following are some examples you can use to write your own classified ad.

Rent to own the house of your choice, a portion of your rent saved for your down payment!

Poor credit okay, minimum $5,000 deposit required. Stop renting and move into a house you choose. Call (123) 456-7890 today!

This advertisement focuses on the two major selling benefits at the same time, the buyer's selection component and the option credit in the headline.

Bruised credit, no credit, no problem!
Pick your home, rent to own AND get help to repair your credit with our unique program. Minimum $5,000 deposit required. The perfect solution for those with good income and credit issues! Call (123) 456-7890 today!

This advertisement focuses on the fact that one doesn't need perfect credit to qualify.

Notice I mentioned the deposit in each ad, regardless of where it's posted. This is a really easy and effective way to pre-qualify people. If a potential applicant sees your ad but doesn't have any money for a deposit and no plans to save up for it, you have just eliminated them before you even started, and saved yourself a lot of time explaining everything when the person is not serious about home ownership.

Often, at this point, people ask me, "Mark, how do you know that person is not serious about home ownership?" I don't want to sound mean or harsh, but the idea of putting money down on something will turn off a lot of people—people you probably don't want to work with, anyhow. Renting to own a house will sound great to this person until they hit the part of the ad that tells them they have to put money into it. If they stop reading there to scan the rest of the rental classifieds, you've just saved yourself the time of explaining the process to someone who wasn't a serious candidate.

The next question I usually get after explaining this is, "What if someone doesn't have money and is serious, but doesn't call because you've scared them off by mentioning a deposit?" Those who are ready will call even if they do not have the money at that time, so if you do get a few phone calls, don't dismiss these people. Take the time to explain the program to them, and let them know they can call back when they are ready in the future. Alternatively, you can put these tenants on a deposit payment plan, in which they give you the deposit in instalments—*before they start looking for a house*. You would put the money in trust with a lawyer and, when the full deposit has been saved, the process can begin. Good candidates will see hope in the things you have told them and begin saving money, or making arrangements to get the money, immediately.

Such was the case with a rent-to-own tenant named Vanessa, whom I spoke with over the phone one afternoon. She was thinking about moving out of her apartment since it was too small and she wanted more room. She didn't have much in savings, not even enough to put down the minimum 2%. But from what she told me, she sounded like a great candidate. I told her to feel free to call back when she had saved up the money and was ready to become a home owner. I was absolutely shocked when she called me back just two days later and said she had a 4% deposit, a house in mind and wanted to get started right away. What happened in those two days between my first conversation with Vanessa and my last? After speaking to her husband, they decided that a rent-to-own was ideal for them. The next day they were driving to the store, and a house they had always loved suddenly had a "for sale" sign on the lawn! Hearts pounding, Vanessa and her husband thought long and hard about their options. And then it clicked—Vanessa had Canada Savings Bonds to which she and her grandparents had been contributing since she was young! Believe it or not, she told me, she had completely forgotten about them. She and her husband decided that her grandparents, who had passed on a few years previous, would be proud of her if she used the savings to buy their first house. And so, she made the call and cashed in all of her Canada Savings Bonds. Voila! Within a few days, she had $14,000 to put toward her deposit, and two months later she and her husband started renting to own the house they had been eyeing for years.

Use your network

Now that you have established yourself as a networking guru (or close to it), it's time to put your network to work. Spread the word at events about your tenant-first rent-to-own opportunity. This is like throwing mud at a wall to see what sticks, and it is incredibly effective. Invariably, the realtor you're speaking with says they had a deal fall apart just yesterday because the client couldn't obtain financing. A mortgage broker you're chatting with tells you a similar story. A woman who owns four apartment buildings turns away applicants all the time because they don't qualify due to poor credit. The janitor who works at the event has a son he's dying to get out of the house. The more you talk about the opportunity, the more possibilities you will discover, and you will be shocked with the results. Within a few conversations, you can have a number of applicants to consider and the only money you have spent is on business cards, which are flying out of your hands. Now, what if you start talking to random people at the grocery store, your gym, the coffee shop ... as you can see, the potential to find tenants is everywhere. You just have to open your mouth and start telling people what you have to offer.

Social networking

In the days of Web 2.0, social networking is a force to be reckoned with. Social networking is one of the best ways to get the word out about anything, including your rent-to-own opportunity. The big three are Facebook, Twitter and LinkedIn.

For rent-to-own purposes, you can post your opportunity in your status for all of your "Facebook Friends" to see. People respond to the status updates and can ask you right there, via a comment on the status or a private email, about rent to own. Also consider starting a group for potential rent-to-own tenants, and invite your friends to join. People who are not listed as your friends can also come across the group and join, and you can send emails to the entire group all at once and post your information on the group "wall." Another way you can use Facebook to your advantage is by targeted pay-per-click advertisements, which show up on the side of the page. You pay when someone clicks your ad and is redirected to a page where they can get more information (this page can also be hosted on Facebook). We will look at pay-per-click advertising in a little more detail in a following section.

Twitter is sort of like Facebook, but focuses only on the "status updates." People "Tweet" a brief thought or, in the case of rent to own an opportunity, which is sent out to all of the person's "followers." People will find you and follow you for many reasons, and it's good Twitter etiquette to reciprocate the contact by following someone who has started following you. Use Twitter to keep your message in front of potential rent-to-own tenants, and make sure you tell them in every post how to reach you for more information.

LinkedIn, essentially, is Facebook for professionals. You can "link" with other professionals by searching a profession, in this case real estate investing, and connect with others for a further expanded network. LinkedIn is a great way to establish a connection with realtors and mortgage professionals who could bring you quality leads.

There are, of course, other social networking sites that can be valuable in a rent-to-own situation, and how much time and effort you put into leads from these tools is entirely up to you. A word of caution though: social networking sites can also be a "time suck," in that as you progress on a particular site, you may spend more time playing Scrabble online than actually doing productive work. Also, there are so many social networking sites these days that one can feel busy with a hectic social networking schedule without accomplishing any practical work. Having said all that, social networking is an inexpensive and convenient way to find potential tenants.

Pay-per-click advertising

Google, Yahoo and other popular search engines all offer something called "pay-per-click advertising." When you search anything in a search engine, usually the first few results you see are "sponsored," meaning someone has paid to have them appear there. Also, on the right-hand side of the results page, there are often additional paid advertisements. Pay-per-click advertising works like this: you create an ad and target who will see it by determining a set of "keywords" ahead of time. In the rent-to-own context, those keywords can be terms such as "rent-to-own Vancouver" or "rent-to-own homes in Barrie." Before you place an ad, you specify what keywords will show a searcher your ad. You are charged when someone clicks on your ad and is sent to a website you designate. When placing an ad, you can set a ceiling on the amount of money you will spend, or the amount of times per day your ad will be shown, so as to prevent a huge, shocking bill at the end of the month. Even with these measures in place, pay-per-click can be expensive if not done right. In fact, it is such an art form these days that there are entire courses dedicated to teaching people how to use this advertising without going broke. If you would like to try pay-per-click advertising, it's well worth your time to get more information and learn how to do it right before you begin, so you don't end up sacrificing your bottom line for the sake of web advertising.

In addition to the web resources and local newspapers, you may also explore posting flyers on bulletin boards in neighborhoods where you wish to invest. Also, if it is legal, you can try putting up posters on lamp posts, using variations of the wording we discussed earlier. If you already have property or know someone who does, consider placing sign posts on the lawn to catch the attention of people walking or driving by.

You have the power to pre-qualify potential tenants with your marketing. If you post your ad at the unemployment office, for example, you can be pretty certain of the type of applicant you will attract. So, decide ahead of time what type of tenant you would like to have. What is their family situation? Where do they work? How much money do they make and what neighborhood appeals to them? Once you have an idea of your ideal tenant, you can begin marketing to this target demographic. Let's say you want your tenants to be a small, growing family who need a bigger place to live and have dreams of home ownership. They have a medium-size dog and two vehicles, and both parents are working. In that case, it would be best to try posting your ads in free local parenting periodicals or community newsletters in an up-and-coming area popular with new parents. You could target a neighborhood with a dog park, for instance, and post signs nearby. If you don't determine ahead of time what kind of tenant you want, you could get anyone—I have a disgusting, smelly mattress to prove it!

Be warned: sometimes it can take a couple of tries to explain to a potential tenant that they get to pick their own house. People are so used to traditional rent-to-own programs that force them to choose from a stock of houses that the first time (and possibly even the second), the appeal of buyer's selection may fall on deaf ears. Rest assured, with some patience on your part, eventually the proverbial light bulb will switch on in their head and they will become so excited. I often hear "Wait, you mean I get to *pick my own house?*" After lengthy explanations over the phone and via email, I can't help but chuckle. The excitement that ensues is usually contagious.

IN REVIEW

You can find tenants by posting ads online, in local newspapers, through social networking sites, pay-per-click advertising and by getting the word out through your network. Pre-screen tenants with your marketing to ensure you are receiving the highest quality applicants possible.

Couple assessed a 24-month rental term, purchase house in just 22 months!

Benjamin and Brenda recently completed a rent to own with me in Oshawa, Ont. The purchase price of the house was $180,000 and they put down a 3% deposit. Their rental term was two years, and they were working with a mortgage broker who was also a specialist in credit repair. They met with their mortgage broker every three months to discuss their next move, and I attended most of the meetings with them. After the meetings I couldn't attend, I followed up with the mortgage broker to make sure Benjamin and Brenda were on track. Boy, were they ever! Their credit steadily improved throughout their rental term, and they were actually able to qualify for a mortgage in 22 months, instead of having to wait the full 24 months. I couldn't have been happier for them! They now own the house, have a child and are some of the proudest home owners one could encounter.

CHAPTER 7

The Tenant Application Form

Now that you have your advertisements posted and potential tenants are beginning to call, there are a few things you need to prepare. The first is a quality application form that potential tenants can fill out in order to be pre-qualified.

A good application will be worth its weight in gold as you search for your ideal tenant. Sample applications can be found online or through the landlord tenant board for each province. Look for a "rental" or "lease" application, as these will most likely prevent you from having to do too much tweaking to design the information collected to be in line with your needs. Search Google for "sample rental application" and you should be provided a number of excellent templates you can use. You can also see the application form I use at www.theversatileinvestor.com, as another option.

A good application will gather all of the information you need from your potential tenant, including contact information, social insurance number and date of birth, the income of all adults who will be living in the house as well as monthly bill payments, debt to loan payments, credit cards and existing mortgages. The application should also tell you about their employment, their work position, salary, employer contact information and length of service with the company.

If the application you use doesn't already have one, make sure you include a spot on the form for the applicant to explain their credit situation, how their circumstances came about and how they plan to change things in the future. We will talk more about the credit story in an upcoming chapter.

Other questions your application can ask are how much the applicant could put toward their deposit, if they already have a house selected, what price range they have in mind and how much they would like to pay each month. There should be adequate space for signatures from all applicants, and the date, since this makes it a legal document.

It is recommended that you have the applicant pull and provide their own credit report, for reasons we'll discuss shortly. If you decide to pull the credit on your own for some reason, your application must include a disclaimer that informs applicants that by signing, they are consenting to a credit check. Without this, you don't have authorization to generate a tenant's credit report, and doing so without their knowledge is against the law.

Tenant Application Form

	Applicant	Co-applicant
Name		
Address		
City/Province		
Postal Code		
Home Phone		
Email		
Date of Birth		
SIN #		
Employer		
Position		
Years at Employer		
Work Phone		
Annual Income		

Tell us a bit about your credit situation and how you got in that situation		

Assets	Value	Liabilities	Balance	Monthly Payment
Real Estate	$	Mortgages	$	$
RRSP	$	Credit Cards	$	$
Stocks & Bonds	$	Other Loans	$	$
Other Assets	$	Total Liability	$	$

How much can you put toward a down payment? _____

Do you already have a house picked out? _____

What price range? _____

By filling out this application and signing, I declare that the application is complete, true and correct, and I herewith give my permission for anyone contacted to release the credit or personal information of the above named applicant(s) to Management or their authorized agents, at any time, for the purposes of entering into and continuing to offer or collect on any agreement and/or credit extended. I further authorize Management or their Authorized Agents to verify the application information including but not limited to obtaining criminal records, contacting creditors, present or former landlords, employers and personal references, whether listed or not, at the time of application and at any time in the future, with regard to any agreement entered into with Management. Any false information will constitute ground for rejection of this application, or Management may at any time immediately terminate any agreement entered into in reliance upon misinformation given on the application.

_____   _____

Applicant Signature   Date

_____   _____

Co-Applicant Signature   Date

I/We authorize a credit check for each applicant (mandatory for completion of the application).

Applicant Initial _____   Co-Applicant Initial _____

If you're going to have the applicant pull their own credit report, you don't need the credit check authorization at the bottom. But if you choose to set up an account with a credit company, you must have this authorization section within the application. Remember to ask how the applicant heard about your rent-to-own program so you can see which advertising methods worked, to help you determine which methods to use next time!

NARROW DOWN THE APPLICANTS

You will receive a number of inquiries, most of which are people simply "tire kicking," who just want information. Explaining rent to own to potential tenants will take a bit of time, and you will find yourself answering many of the same questions over and over. You will soon start to be able to tell the real applicants from the rest and will be able to streamline the conversations. If you develop a website, typical questions can be answered in a "frequently asked questions" section. Out of the "tire kickers," a few applicants will emerge as more serious than others. These are the applicants you will want to pursue.

Ask them questions not just about their application, but also about other parts of their lives. For example, if you know your applicant is a plumber and you ask him how he likes his job, you may learn he actually hates it and is thinking about quitting. If you're not sure what to be asking a potential tenant, consider this their "interview." Ask a couple how long they have been together, and what has brought on their credit situation. Have they been thinking of home ownership for long? What motivates them to buy, and why do they like the area they're looking at? What are their plans for the future?

LOOK FOR THE THREE QS

While meeting with potential tenants, you should look for three things in particular, which I like to refer to as the three Qs.

Quality

A quality tenant is not just someone who looks good on paper or can afford the rent to own. A quality tenant also must give you a good feeling that their motivations for buying a house are genuine and that they have a real desire to better their situation. They have good reason for their credit situation, and are demonstrably motivated to change their situation for the better. They're willing to commit completely to a credit repair program, and most likely have begun making those steps. Regardless of how their current circumstances came about, a quality tenant is dedicated to repairing their credit and is ready for home ownership.

A quality tenant is not one to nickel-and-dime. Rather, they are easy to deal with and are not opposed to doing the things it takes to obtain their ideal house, such as paying for a home inspection, providing references and gathering a strong deposit. Those who are "quality" are easy to work with and eager to get the deal underway.

Qualified

Of course, they should also be qualified, meaning that they have enough money to cover all of their old debts as well as their new lease payment. If someone is not qualified and you put them in a rent-to-own situation, you are not doing either of you any favors. If a potential tenant is applying based on income they think, wish or assume is going to be coming their way, they are *not qualified*! At least, they're not qualified now—but they will be when that money appears. Never enter a rent-to-own agreement with someone who is not qualified, even if that means they are not *yet* qualified. Advise them to wait until the money they're waiting for comes in and then they can re-apply.

Quick to Move

Naturally, when making a decision about renting to own, a tenant does need to think it over. However, the tenant-first scenario will eliminate a lot of the "musing" time that plagues the traditional rent-to-own strategy. Why? Because your tenants are choosing their own house, of course! They're not just applying to see how the program works. An ideal tenant already knows they want to purchase a house, and they just have to find it. This doesn't mean you shouldn't work with those who need time to mull it over, but you should focus on working with the people who are motivated. If the others mull it over and come back, ready to act, it was meant to be. When applicants are submitting their supporting documents (which will be outlined for you later) they are very quick to act. The ideal tenant's application is also complete and you don't have to chase them for additional information. Not only will this behavior save you time and stress in the beginning, it will also give you some insight as to how a potential tenant will act in the future.

Our friend Tim uses these techniques to find a number of potential tenants, all of which wish to apply for his tenant-first rent-to-own program. With the knowledge of what to look for in a tenant, he is ready to move on to the next step—learning how to qualify an applicant. Let's follow the process with him, shall we?

IN REVIEW

Find a quality application you can use over and over. Have the applicant pull their own credit report and submit it to you. Narrow down applicants by eliminating "tire kickers" and by using the three Qs: quality, qualified and quick to move.

Deal provides stunning 70% return on investment!

One of my favorite deals was in Fort McMurray, Alta. The husband worked in the oil sands, and the house they wanted to buy cost $575,000. The tenants put down a large deposit of 4%, and their monthly lease payment was calculated by multiplying the purchase price by .0085. It's common to find extremely high return on houses with high purchase prices. The investor on this deal, a friend with whom I work very closely, makes a whopping $2,500 in positive monthly cash flow from just this one property!

CHAPTER 8

Qualifying Applicants

Tim is delighted when he opens his email one morning to find a number of responses to a recent ad he posted online for rent to own. He pre-screens the potential applicants and narrows it to two couples with whom he can work: Jonathan and Cindy, and Gary and Rita. Now he needs to figure out if the two couples qualify.

HOW TO QUALIFY AN APPLICANT

Once initial contact with a potential applicant is made, send them an application form. Which form you use is up to you, and I have provided one I like to use at the back of this book and a working copy online at www.theversatile-investor.com in a special section exclusive to readers of *Investing Rent-to-own Property*. You will find that in some cases, there will be two applicants but only one income can be used to determine if they are qualified, as is the case if one of the applicants is unemployed, self-employed and cannot prove income, or is on government benefits such as maternity leave. Even in such cases, both people must fill out the application, since there will be two primary tenants. Self-employed people can prove income by showing their most recent income tax return.

You also need to request that a copy of their credit report accompany their application. We will discuss this further in Chapter 10, when we look at credit reports in depth.

Once you have received the application from the tenant, make sure it is complete and signed, and discuss any omissions. To qualify your applicant, there are essentially four points (and a secret fifth) to take into consideration:

1. Income

2. Credit story

3. Employment

4. Debt coverage ratio (gross debt service/total debt service)

5. The Secret Fifth Point of Qualification

To illustrate, let's check back in with Jonathan and Cindy. If you remember, Jonathan is our divorcee who recently declared bankruptcy. Cindy is a flight attendant who was a victim of identity theft. As it turns out, Jonathan and Cindy are looking for a house to rent that will be big enough for the family they plan to start. They also want to get a dog in the near future and so would like to have a fenced-in back yard. Jonathan and Cindy have a neighborhood in mind where the average selling price is $450,000.

Income

Of course, the first thing you should consider is the applicant's income. Consider all sources of income, not just that earned from a traditional job. Maybe they operate a small side business from home, or there's some rental income from a relative living with them. If they are using rental income, they have to demonstrate a legal apartment. However, if they do have someone living with them, *their* income can be taken into account for the total household income, provided the renter is on the application. Child benefit and other government benefits also count toward income.

If you remember, Jonathan's luck had recently changed on the job front, and he got a great job on an oil rig paying $96,000 a year. Cindy has worked as a flight attendant for a few years, and is now making $36,000 annually. She also receives royalties from a song she wrote when she was younger, which amounts to about $200 per month. All together, they make $134,400 gross.

Credit Story

Around 90% of people who take advantage of a rent to own do so because their credit scores are low, and most lenders look only at credit scores to determine approval, and don't go any further. When you are considering an applicant, however, you have the power to dig a little deeper and find out more about the situation before you make a decision on a potential tenant.

There is more to an applicant's credit story than just their credit score (although that does play a big part). The credit story explains how the applicant's situation came about, encompassing both the information from their credit bureau and what they tell you during your "interviewing." This is why I say you need to take into account their credit *story* and not just their score. Take the time to learn about each applicant's past; in essence, have them tell you the "story" of how they arrived in their current situation.

To keep things simple, have your applicants provide their own credit reports. They can go to Equifax's consumer site, www.econsumer.equifax.ca, and pull a copy of the report online for a small fee. Having the applicant pull their own report has two main benefits: first, you will not have to register with a company to pull credit, or incur the expense of membership with one of the major credit companies. Also, having the applicant pull their own report is the first step in the credit repair program. A number of different reports can be pulled, some of which detail only the open accounts on their report and do not disclose the credit score or history. Make sure you advise your applicant to choose the report that includes their credit score. If they're reluctant to take this step, they may have saved you a lot of time by disqualifying themselves!

If you remember, we have already heard Jonathan and Cindy's credit story—Jonathan's messy divorce and bankruptcy, and Cindy's identity theft. They are serious about repairing their credit, and have already taken the first steps to doing this on their own. We will look closer at their credit in the next chapter, and see if Jonathan and Cindy's credit can be repaired within a reasonable rental period.

Employment

When looking for your ideal tenant, verifying their employment is key. Request a job letter from each applicant's employer which should state the length of time they have been in the position and their salary. In the meantime, as we run the numbers to determine if they're pre-approved, look at three factors. First, ask about their job tenure. How long have they worked at their current job? What is their annual gross salary? If they have been in their current job for less than two years, where did they work before? Why did they leave? How long were they employed by the previous company? How much did they make? What made them choose their new position?

In addition to tenure, also consider their income. Are they at the top end of the spectrum for their position, or the bottom? Have they received regular pay increases?

Lastly, when it comes to employment, also consider the industry they're in. Is it healthy, or is there a good chance they may lose their job in the near future? Is their industry unionized? If laid off, they may not qualify for a mortgage at the end of the term if their rental term is too short, their new job (if they get one in time) may not pay as much, or the bank may not accept shorter job tenure.

Debt coverage ratio (gross debt service/total debt service)

Now that we know that Jonathan and Cindy have good income and we like their credit story, it's time to bust out your calculator. Our next step is to run some figures, which will determine whether the applicants can afford a rent to own and how much they can spend on monthly lease payments when factored in with their other debt payments. These calculations will also tell you the maximum they can afford to pay for a house. Fortunately, because of the tenant-first strategy, we have the ability to tell applicants what they can afford ahead of time, so not everyone needs to be declined because of income. To do this we must determine their DSCR/DCR by calculating GDS and TDS. Let's look at what these four acronyms mean:

- DCR: Debt Coverage Ratio

- DSCR: Debt Service Coverage Ratio

For our purposes, DCR and DSCR mean the same thing—the ratio of money available to put toward servicing interest, principal and lease payments. Or, in layman's terms, whether the applicant has enough funds to cover all existing debt, plus their new lease payment on the property they will be renting to own. DCR can be determined using the following ratios:

- GDS: Gross Debt Service Ratio

GDS is used to determine whether an applicant is already in too much debt, and the Canadian Mortgage and Housing Corporation (CMHC) recommends using GDS to determine the maximum home-related expenses one can afford each month. These expenses include principal, interest, taxes and heating. GDS is calculated on gross income (the amount one makes monthly before taxes are deducted) and shouldn't be more than 32% of the applicant's monthly income. So, to calculate GDS, add all of the household income and multiply the total by 0.32. When calculating the numbers, GDS is something to keep in mind, but you should focus on the other ratio, TDS, which will give you a complete analysis of their debt ratio.

- TDS: Total Debt Service Ratio

TDS refers to the total amount of debt load one can carry each month. In layman's terms, TDS encompasses all of the payments—the *total* debt, not just those related to housing. The additions could include a car payment, loans, credit cards or lines of credit. This should be no more than 40% of one's monthly income, and again calculated on gross income. To determine TDS, add the total monthly household income and multiply by .40. That is the total allowable debt ratio an applicant can afford each month.

Wow, how is that for a slew of acronyms and calculations! Don't worry, we're going to work with these calculations a bit here, and put our friends Jonathan and Cindy to the test to see what they can afford.

PRACTICE MAKES PERFECT

Just like any skill, you will want to practise these calculations with some living examples until it comes easily to you—and it will. Eventually you might even be able to run these numbers in your head. If you can, I salute you. For the rest of us, it's a good idea to carry around our trusty PDAs or pocket calculators.

RUNNING THE NUMBERS

It's important to remember that when you're running the numbers for a potential rent-to-own tenant, you should qualify them on their situation now *and* at the end of the rental period to ensure they will be able to afford the buy-out price.

Let's return to Jonathan and Cindy, our rental applicants. We'll take the information we gathered about them while speaking with them in the initial phase of the qualification and use it for our calculations.

Jonathan makes $96,000 per year, and Cindy pulls in $36,000. They receive another $2,400 annually from Cindy's music royalties. In total, they make $134,400 per year gross income, or $11,200 per month. GDS is calculated at 32% and TDS at 40%. The numbers look like this:

GDS: $11,200/month x .32 = $3,584

This is the amount they can spend each month on their household expenses, including the lease payments.

TDS: $11,200/month x .40 = $4,480

This is the amount they can have going to their total debt each month.

Based on these calculations, you must look at their debts as they have outlined on their application form. Cindy has a truck payment each month of $438 and a credit card with a $4,000 balance, her minimum payment being $350 a month. The couple has a line of credit to which they pay $356 per month. These three monthly debt payments total $1,144.00, and that amount should be subtracted from the TDS calculation of $4,480 a month, leaving them with $3,336 they can put toward a lease. Can they afford a $450,000 house, as they originally stated they wanted?

Depending on the city or town in which an applicant is looking to buy, I calculate their lease payments by multiplying the purchase price of the house by between .008 and .0095. On the low end, this would put their monthly lease payments at $3,600. Unfortunately, with the truck, credit card and line of credit payments they have to make each month, Jonathan and Cindy will not be able to afford a $450,000 house.

ALL IS NOT LOST

The fact that Jonathan and Cindy don't make enough money to service both a lease payment and their monthly debt for a $450,000 house doesn't mean they can't do a rent to own. Because they are choosing their house, this simply means we have to tell them how much they *can* afford.

You can quickly determine how much an applicant can afford by multiplying their yearly income by three. This is a very basic and safe calculation to ensure that, providing they make the same money at the end of the rental term, even if interest rates go up, they will still be able to purchase the property in a couple of years. So, in Jonathan and Cindy's case, we calculate:

Total gross yearly income: $134,400 x 3 = $403,200

Now we can return to Jonathan and Cindy and tell them they're approved for a rent to own, but the purchase price of the house must be no more than $400,000. Knowing how much they can spend, the couple can now go shopping, something Cindy has proven very skilled at in the past.

QUALIFICATION AT THE END OF THE RENTAL TERM

We're not through yet. There's one more factor we must take into consideration: the buy-back amount. An applicant must also qualify for the lease at the end of the rental term. Qualifying an applicant based solely on the purchase price now is truly doing yourself, as well as the applicant, a disservice. Remember, your exit strategy for your investment is to sell the property to the tenant at the end of the rental term, yielding you your full return on investment. If they cannot afford to buy the house in the end, entering a rent to own with the applicant is setting everyone up for disaster.

Depending on the area and the housing market, I usually calculate the appreciation rate between 6 and 9% per year. To determine the best appreciation rate, consider the history of the area over the past five years and projected future trends. You will have to do your homework here, but if you have done your due diligence (which we will talk about a bit more in the next chapter) you should have a good idea what a reasonable appreciation rate might be. You can also use your financial analysis spreadsheet to juggle the numbers to ensure the appreciation rate will ultimately give you the return on investment you're looking for.

Calculating based on the purchase price of $400,000 and a low apprecia-
tion rate of 6% compounded each year for a three-year rental term, will Jonathan and Cindy qualify at the end of the rental term?

$400,000 x 1.06 (6% appreciation for the first year) = $424,000 x 1.06 (6% appreciation for the second year) = $449,440 x 1.06 (you guessed it! 6% apprecia-
tion for the third year) = $476,406.

Juggle the new purchase price of $476,406 with a mortgage rate of 6% on a
25-year amortization, and their mortgage payment works out to be $3,048.08.
We originally said that their allowable TDS was $4,480. Provided Jonathan
and Cindy stick to their repayment plan of their truck loan, credit cards and
line of credit, they will most definitely be able to afford the final purchase price
at the end of the rental term.

WHEN THE TENANT ALREADY OWNS THEIR HOME

This strategy also allows you to work with another type of tenant—those who
already own their home.

Remember Gary and Rita, the home owners who, in spite of appearances,
were actually spread too thin, financially? Gary and Rita can benefit from rent
to own by having someone purchase their property so they will not lose their
home. They have sold their timeshare in Cabo San Lucas and their lifetime
memberships to the golf club, which has yielded some money and eased their
situation. Gary reluctantly sold his motorboat, and Rita downsized her SUV to
a used mid-size vehicle, which she paid for outright, eliminating her monthly
payment. They have taken a step in the right direction, but still need someone
to buy their house to keep them from going under.

Gary and Rita's situation is different from Jonathan and Cindy's rent to
own because they already own their house, and therefore have already accumulated equity in the property. Equity is a powerful thing! They owe $550,000
on their house, but would like to get a bit extra to help them pay off their consolidation loan and to put down a 5% deposit. Can Tim do this? He's not sure

at the start, so he orders an appraisal on the house (which I recommend any time you're doing a rent to own with a tenant who already owns their home). To Tim's delight, the appraisal comes back at $650,000! Not wanting Gary and Rita's payments to be too high for them, Tim decides to purchase the property for $600,000, giving Gary and Rita an extra $50,000 to put toward their deposit and pay off debt. In this case, when the tenant already has equity in the home they would like to use toward their deposit, you need to have a letter of direction drawn up for the funds to be dispersed to you at the time of the sale. Your real estate lawyer can tell you more about letters of direction and what, specifically, is involved in this process.

When a tenant puts down a large deposit, it provides me with the ability to bring the lease payments down while still making a good return and monthly cash flow. Whether you decide to follow suit is up to you, but it's worth considering as a way to negotiate larger deposits from your tenants. Tim agrees with this method of thinking, and drops Gary and Rita's monthly rental calculation from .0085 to .0075.

The big question now is: can Gary and Rita afford to lease their home for $600,000, and if they do, will it truly benefit them in the end?

To juggle the numbers for Gary and Rita, we will again use the 6% appreciation rate for each year, assuming they will be doing a three-year rental term.

Gary makes $120,000 per year, and Rita, who volunteers her time, doesn't have an income. Their income is too much to qualify for the Canadian Child Tax Benefit, so in total they make $120,000 per year gross, or $10,000 per month. GDS is calculated at 32% and TDS at 40%. The numbers look like this:

GDS: $10,000/month x .32 = $3,200

That is the amount they can spend each month on their household expenses, including the lease payments, but again we will not focus on GDS as much as the next calculation, the TDS.

TDS: $10,000/month x .40 = $4,000

As with Jonathan and Cindy, we then look at the debt they have outlined in their application. They have already paid off a number of their debts and sold some of their luxuries. They also got a consolidation loan from their bank, to which they pay $600 per month. Their current TDS is $4,000 per month, minus the $600 debt repayment, which leaves them $3,400 per month to put toward their lease payment. Can their current income support the $550,000 rent to own of their own house?

Tim has decided to calculate Gary and Rita's a monthly rental payment at .0075. Keep in mind, this is hypothetical, because you won't know for sure whether that number will give you the return on investment you're looking for until you run the numbers through a financial analysis spreadsheet, which we will look at more closely in the next chapter. At this point, we are simply pre-qualifying them, in a sense, to see if rent to own is right for them. Here is the calculation:

$600,000 x .0075 = $4,500/month

As it stands, they are over on their TDS. But, Gary and Rita are ideal rent-to-own tenants, and their motivation for doing a rent to own is a powerful one—they want to keep their house. They have already taken steps in the right direction with their consolidation loan, which proves they are committed. We don't want them to get away if we can help it! So, since we are creative investors who like to look outside the box, on our next phone call, we offer a suggestion. They need to bring in more income to qualify, and there are many ways to do that. Gary agrees to ask for a raise at work, but he is not hopeful about the outcome. Rita's connections offer her an opportunity to work for a not-for-profit agency. She was looking for a new challenge and the extra income will save their family home. Within a month, she is working and making $45,000 per year, boosting the couple's income by $3,750 per month. The job tenure is short, but she has a letter from her employer stating she is a valuable member of the team and they don't see her employment changing in the future. Do they now qualify? You betcha, and they have also shown a resilience and commitment to the house that will help any investor sleep well at night.

The Secret Fifth Point of Qualification

There is one more aspect to take into consideration when qualifying a tenant: your instinct. You will get a gut feeling about a tenant when you speak with them, either good or bad. Asking the applicant questions about their motives and their situation will tell you a lot, but when it comes down to it, if you have a bad feeling about someone despite their perfect application, chances are there is a reason for it.

Now, let's get something straight on this point. When I say you need to trust your "gut feeling," I don't mean you should approve someone just because you like them. For this secret fifth point of qualification to work, you must remove all emotion from your decision. Chances are, as you begin speaking to potential tenants, you will run into one or two that you genuinely like. You are almost guaranteed to hear some horrible stories, since often the reason an applicant is in the situation is because of something beyond their control. You will hear stories from completely innocent people about how their identities were stolen, and their lives ruined from no fault of their own. You will learn of a person's four-year struggle with cancer. And, unfortunately, you will hear about spouses dying, nasty divorces and many other horrible situations. It is human nature to pity people, to feel badly for them and to try to help them. As hard as it may be, you will need to distance yourself from the emotion of an investment and focus on the figures alone. If they don't qualify but you approve them anyway because you feel badly for them, you are setting yourself up for disaster. When I talk about "gut feeling," I mean the little twinge in your stomach that tells you something is not right, the tiny sideways glance you noticed that made you wonder if an applicant is telling the whole truth. If you quiet the emotion, the excitement, fear or pity, your instincts will provide direction when something is not right, something you can't quite put your finger on. Don't discount your gut feeling, either positive or negative. Trust your instincts to steer you in the right direction about the people with whom you are going to do business, but make sure it's your gut you are paying attention to and not your heart.

Approving an applicant

One of the easiest ways to let an applicant know they are pre-approved is by providing an approval letter. This will simply state that the applicant has been pre-approved, and that they need to provide further documentation to take the rent-to-own process to the next step. Include all of your contact information, and whether you would like the applicant to email or fax the documents to you. When sending the approval letter or any other contract or document to the applicant, it is advisable to use a PDF. This Portable Document Format turns a regular word processing file, which can be altered, into an unchangeable document. While we hope our applicants will not change anything on a contract or document without first discussing it with us, it's a good idea to take the precaution and format any official correspondence into a PDF file. PDF also looks a lot more professional than simply sending a regular Word document.

Adobe provides software with which one can "PDF" pretty much any type of file. You can purchase Adobe software if you prefer, but there are also low- or no-cost methods for "PDF-ing" a file. PDF995 is free software that's easy to use and can be downloaded in minutes. In your word processing document, you print the file as you usually would, but instead of specifying your printer as the destination, you would choose the "PDF" option. No paper actually comes out of your printer, but when the process is complete you have a PDF version of your original document.

You can certainly use your own wording for the approval letter, but you are welcome to base your approval letter on the text I personally use.

Congratulations!

You have been pre-approved, but the approval process is not yet complete. Please begin gathering the following documents and return them as soon as possible:

- ❑ 20xx and 20xx NOAs
- ❑ 20xx and 20xx T4s
- ❑ Job letter for all applicants and all jobs

❏ T1 for self-employed persons
❏ 2 Pieces of ID for each applicant, with at least 1 photo ID

Fax the above documents to (123) 456-7890 or email them to my-email@awesomewebhoster.com

Sincerely,

Your Name

Company Name (if applicable)
Phone: (123) 456-7890
Fax: (123) 456-7890

Declining an applicant

There will be times when you need to decline an applicant. It might be because their income is not high enough, the lease payment would put them over their allowed TDS ratio or because you have simply chosen not to work with the applicant. You can relay the news over the phone or in person, or you may choose to issue a standard decline letter, which outlines the reasons they are not eligible for your rent-to-own program.

In the decline letter, consider explaining the reasons for declining the applicant. If it's an issue of their TDS ratio or low income, the applicant will benefit from knowing the reason they're not eligible now, and may be able to fix the issues and reapply later. As always, you can create your own decline letter, but you are welcome to adopt the following sample.

Dear (applicant),

Unfortunately, you do not qualify for rent to own at this time. After examining your financial circumstances, we have determined that your current debt ratio is too high to allow the monthly lease payment needed for a rent-to-own property. The allowable amount of income that can go toward debt is 40%. Due to the _____ (debt payments), adding a lease payment would create a situation in which you are over the allowable TDS ratio. If these circumstances change, we welcome you to reapply.

Thank you for your application, and we hope to work with you in the future.
Sincerely,
Your Name

Company Name (if applicable)
Phone: (123) 456-7890
Fax: (123) 456-7890

IN REVIEW

Qualify an applicant by looking at their income, credit story, employment, TDS/GDS and by trusting your gut feeling when you suspect something is wrong. Send an approved applicant a letter that explains they are pre-qualified and requests supporting documents. When declining an applicant, a letter can also be issued or you can decline them in person or over the phone. Whenever possible, explain why they've been declined and tell them what they can do to fix the issues if they would like to reapply in the future. Never close the door on someone, because they could be a valuable tenant in the future.

Couple trades big house for peace of mind

A sure sign of a bad economy, many people are not just looking to become home owners, but are instead looking for help to save their homes. This was the case with the Columbos. Mr. Columbo was in backyard pool sales, an industry that had grossed him and his family more than $250,000 a year in the past. The markets changed, suddenly pools were a luxury and his sales plummeted. He's now making only $125,000 per year. His wife was not working due to medical reasons, and the Columbos found they were quickly behind on everything, and didn't see a light at the end of the tunnel. They had to do something, and quick, or they would soon find their house taken by the bank, their belongings repossessed and their credit ruined. Originally, we looked at purchasing their existing house for them and then allowing them to rent to own it back on a three-year term. This would give them enough time to pay off their other loans and debts. But the husband's income alone was no longer enough to support the mortgage payment, let alone a lease payment. The bank was not being helpful in any way, so I set them up with one of my trusted realtors and a mortgage broker who is incredibly knowledgeable in alternative financing solutions. With all of us drafting up possible fixes, the true solution became clear: with the bank so uncooperative, the Columbos had no negotiation power. The bank would take their house, that was inevitable, as they had a non-recourse loan, and the bank would recoup its money from CMHC. The Columbos had resigned to their fate—they would have to sell their family home. But rather than end up on the street (or, as Mr. Columbo joked, living in one of his backyard pools), we set them up with a rent to own on a property that was a significantly lower purchase price. His decreased income at its lowest point supported the smaller house (which, in the city where they lived was no shack, let me tell you!). When their income bounced back up, they would quickly pay off their other debts and probably even be able to buy out early. The Columbos were reluctant to leave their family home, but knew that was what they had to do to survive. At the time of writing, they have just begun their rental term in the downsized house. Both of their faces are lighter, and I even saw Mr. Columbo crack a smile—finally! The stress had become so great that no property was worth the health issues it was creating for both of them. A smaller house in this case meant greater peace of mind at a time when peace of mind is hard to come by.

# CHAPTER 9

Doing Your Due Diligence

We have a qualified tenant, but our job does not end there. Now we must do our due diligence and make sure everything our applicants have told us is legitimate. The onus is on you, the investor, to cover your bases and verify all the information. This is for your own protection, and who better to protect yourself than you? Taking the time and effort to verify all of the information provided to you will not only ensure a smooth transaction, it will also increase your confidence in the deal, allowing you to move forward without worry about anything going wrong.

There are many different ways to perform due diligence with a rent-to-own program, and you may feel as though you need more information from the applicant than what we touch on here. If this happens, ask the applicant for the additional documents or proof you need, and make sure they are disclosing all of the facts of their circumstances.

When you tell your applicant they are "pre-approved," you must request a number of documents from them, including:

- Job Letters for each applicant verifying employment
- Notice of Assessments for the last two years for all applicants
- T4s for the past two years for all applicants
- Two recent pay stubs for each applicant
- A copy of their credit report (you should have requested this earlier, before pre-approving them, but you will use it during your due diligence, so make sure you have it handy!)

THE JOB LETTER

Each applicant should provide you with a job letter from their employer, which outlines that, in fact, they are employed there, for how long and their rate of pay. Job letters are a standard request from employees these days, and can be obtained by contacting the human resources department or speaking with their superior. The job letter will also state a contact's name and phone number if you need any more information. This will come in handy as we are completing our due diligence.

NOTICE OF ASSESSMENT

The Notice of Assessment, or NOA, is a document provided from the government after a tax return is filed. Have each applicant provide their notice of assessment for the past two years to prove their income and if they have back taxes owing. Of course, sometimes their previous notice of assessment shows less income than what they're currently making, as is the case when a pay raise is received or a new position obtained. The NOA is a good way to verify income, but obtaining these documents has an even more important role: proving that the applicants have filed their taxes for the past two years. If a tax payer owes money to the government, this is always the first priority for payment, which can leave a landlord in a sticky situation if the government comes to collect through "involuntary" means. Making sure these documents are in order and the tenant has filed their taxes (and paid, if they owe) is another way you, the investor, must protect yourself. If the applicant doesn't have their NOAs for the past two years but has filed their taxes, they can request a copy from Canada Revenue Agency. This usually takes 10 business days. If the applicant has not yet filed their taxes for the past two years, insist they do so before the process goes any further and save yourself a world of potential stress later on.

T4s

No doubt you have seen your own T4 when you file your taxes each year. A T4 is issued by an employer, and is used by a tax payer when they file their taxes to complete all the information on the return. Request the past two years of T4s from a potential tenant so you can verify the income they're claiming in their application. All applicants should provide T4s for all of their jobs in the past two years. As with the NOAs, if they do not have their T4s, they can request to have them sent from the government, and it usually takes about 10 business days.

T1s

If an applicant is self-employed, they will not have T4s. Instead, request the T1 forms for the last two years of their tax return. The T1 general form is the place where the person's income is declared.

IDENTIFICATION

Request two pieces of identification for each applicant, at least one being photo ID. The applicant can photocopy or scan the identification and send it to you, but make sure you specify the forms of identification are readable, as sometimes photocopies and scans don't come through as clearly as regular scans.

PAY STUBS

Next in our arsenal of paperwork, request the two most recent pay stubs from each applicant. These will not only ensure that the applicant is gainfully employed, but will also prove to you that each applicant is making income they claim on their application.

THE CREDIT BUREAU

You will need to see the credit bureau of each applicant for two reasons. First, you need to see their credit score to determine their rental term and to make sure their credit is repairable. Second, you must cross-reference the debt load they declared on their application with the information found in their credit report to ensure they have disclosed a true account of their current debt.

Having the applicant pull their own bureau will keep you from having to register with a credit company, which is a lengthy and expensive process with recurring fees. In addition, having the applicant pull their own report is the first step in any credit repair process; after all, if a tenant doesn't know what's on their bureau, they cannot take the necessary steps to fix it. They need to become familiar with the process of pulling their own credit as they will be re-viewing it at least every three months with you or their designated credit repair specialist. If they are unwilling to pull their own credit and provide it to you, it's a sure sign that something is wrong. It's also advisable to have them register for a monthly monitoring plan, which most credit companies offer. By hav-ing the tenant pull their own bureau, you are empowering them toward their own credit repair. An added benefit to the applicant is that when they request their own credit report, it doesn't count as a "hit" on their credit, whereas if you make the request, it will show on their record. Too many requests equals a lower credit score, which is something no applicant needs while on the path of credit restoration. In the next chapter, we'll look at assessing a credit report much closer.

EMPLOYMENT VERIFICATION/REFERENCE CHECK

You owe it to yourself to check references, just as an employer would check the references of a job applicant. Call their employers to make sure their employ-ment is valid. Many investors have stories about an applicant submitting a job letter with a false contact name and number. The contact turned out to be the applicant's friend, and a simple phone call showed the applicant had drafted a phoney job letter to try to pull the wool over the investor's eyes. When call-ing to verify the job, don't automatically dial the number provided on the let-ter. Instead, dial the main switchboard, which can usually be found simply by looking up the company in the phone book, at www.canada411.com or on the company's website. Ask for the human resources department.

In doing your due diligence, you may want to get further proof of income. Additional documents you may request include bank statements and references from former landlords. If you are feeling unsure of any part of their applica-tion, go ahead and make the request, if for no other reason than to set your mind at ease. If the applicant is being entirely truthful with you, they will have no problem backing up their claims.

It can take applicants time to find and gather the requested documents, especially if they have to request to have them sent from the government. Make sure you give the applicants adequate time to source the information, and as they're gathering these documents you can be moving on to the next step. Once you have everything you need, you can get down to the nitty gritty of doing your due diligence. Verify they have filed their taxes, and if they owed, that they have paid. Use the T4s provided to confirm their income from the past two years and look at their current pay stubs to make sure their income is as they stated on the application.

Checking back in with our old pal Tim, he has been very thorough in his due diligence. He had a good chat with Gary's employer, and feels even more confident about having Jonathan and Cindy as tenants after speaking with their current landlord, who gave the couple nothing but rave reviews.

IN REVIEW

Do your due diligence to protect yourself! Always follow up job letters with a phone call to the employer. If the applicant doesn't have all of the required documents, advise them to begin gathering them immediately.

Join-venture investor switches strategies, lives happily ever after

One investor I deal with, Barry, dealt with traditional rental properties exclusively, and mostly multi-family units. As any seasoned investor can attest, these can require a lot of work. The cash flow from Barry's property was not in the red, but it was not where he wanted it to be. The return on investment and capital appreciation of the tenant-first rent-to-own strategy was appealing to Barry, so he set about switching his investment strategy. Barry primarily invests with joint-venture partners, and he finds this strategy very easy to sell to them. Since he began tenant-first rent-to-own investing a year ago, Barry has tripled his monthly cash flow and he and his JV partners are very, very happy with their returns.

CHAPTER 10

What Credit Bureau Information Can Tell You

Viewing the credit bureau is a very important step in performing your due diligence. Implementing a rent-to-own strategy means you will be dealing mostly with people with bruised credit, consumer proposals and previous bankruptcies. Still, you need to scour an applicant's credit report for a couple of reasons, but mainly to protect your interests.

Reading a credit report is a book in itself. This is a time when your relationship with a mortgage professional or credit repair specialist will really serve you well. Your mortgage professional can help you look at a credit report in detail, and advise you of any red flags. Here's a crash course on the standard things to watch out for when analyzing an applicant's credit report.

A credit score is referred to by a number of terms these days, including "bureau," "FICO score" and "beacon score," but they all mean one thing: the overall rating a person receives to inform credit lenders and other professionals of a person's likeliness to repay extended credit, or more aptly, a person's likeliness to default on payments.

A credit score is made up of a number of components, which break down like this:

- 35%—past payment history. This portion of the score will be affected by late payments, past due accounts and bankruptcies, to name a few.

- 30%—credit owing. This includes total amounts owed on accounts such as credit cards and loans, and is also affected by the ratio of credit available to credit used. In the case of a credit card, this would mean the amount of a balance being carried versus their actual limit.

- 15%—length of time credit has been established. Those who have new credit, such as people new to the country or those who have never used credit, will be negatively affected in this area. The longer the person has used credit, the better this portion of their score will be.

- 10%—searches and acquisition of credit. This includes the number of "hits" on a credit bureau. The more hits, the worse this portion will be affected. The number of "new" accounts will also affect this section of the score.

- 10%—types of credit a person has established. Included in this ratio are the various types of credit the person has used.

A credit score in the low 500s can be repaired within three years, a score in the high 500s to low 600s would need a two-year term, and anything between about 640 and 680 would require one year. One-year terms are rare in the rent-to-own world, simply because with a good mortgage broker, the average credit-challenged person can obtain a mortgage with a 680 score or higher. A credit score is considered good when it is around 680 and excellent over 700. Here is the general rule I like to follow:

- 560 or less: three-year term
- 560 to 620: two-year term
- 620 and up: one-year term

This information is solely for your background knowledge, as it will not be broken down in such a way when you are looking at a credit report.

Each account on the credit report will be one of three possible account types:

- "I" stands for "instalment" credit, which means the person was given credit to be repaid in instalments, such as a car loan. This loan is repaid regularly in fixed amounts for a predetermined period of time.

- "R" stands for "revolving" credit, which means that payment amounts vary but are paid on a regular basis depending on the balance on the account, as is the case with a credit card.

1. "O" stands for "open" credit, where money is borrowed as needed up to a certain amount, as in a line of credit.

Beside these letters you will see a number between 0 and 9, 0 meaning that nothing has happened on that account yet. The number 1 represents payments being made within 30 days of the due date. Two, three, four and so on show any time longer than that, perhaps a late payment has taken place. An "R7" will show up if the client has taken a consolidation loan. The number 9 is the one you need to watch out for most. A "9" indicates that the payments have not been made for a very long time, and have been written off by the credit issuer.

Question any recent non-payments on the bureau, and find out why the applicant has not been paying their bills recently.

Bankruptcies are another entity to watch out for, as a person needs two years after the date of discharge from the bankruptcy (not the date it was declared), which will have a huge bearing on the rental term the applicant needs to clean up their credit. Also, keep an eye out for any judgments or liens.

Looking at Jonathan and Cindy's credit reports, we find that Jonathan was fully honest with us about the extent of his situation. He did, in fact, declare bankruptcy, which shows on his bureau. His bankruptcy was discharged three months ago. Cindy was also truthful about her situation. It's clear from her credit report that she has been the victim of identity theft. In the span of two days, her bureau was pulled more than 30 times by potential credit lenders, everything from cell phone companies to credit cards to automotive dealers. There were also 16 new accounts opened in her name in that time, all of which carry a balance of more than $10,000! Naturally, she is not liable for all of that money, but her score will suffer even after the accounts are closed. Cindy is diligent, constantly following up with the major credit reporting bureaus and monitoring her credit activity, but it is definitely going to take some time to get her credit back to where it was before.

Jonathan's score is 538 and Cindy's is 515. The couple will benefit from a longer term as they need lots of time to repair their credit, so we will give them a three-year term. If Jonathan and Cindy can restore it sooner, they can buy out early. We want to create a win/win situation for everyone, and if they can buy out early, consider giving them a discount on their purchase price, providing you're making the same return on investment.

Gary and Rita's situation is a bit different. Their credit has been only mildly affected by their financial situation; a few late payments here, a few missed payments there. When they bring us their credit reports, the first thing we see is that Gary's credit score is 620. Rita's score comes in a bit lower, at 580. What happened? Well, it seems Rita was not as good a juggler as she appeared. When deciding where their money would go each month, some accounts fell through the cracks. Rita always paid the big accounts, the "important" ones that were under both of their names. Feeling as though their financial troubles were the result of her mismanagement, when a payment had to be missed Rita selflessly sacrificed the accounts that were under her name alone. All of this is understandable, but should it really leave Rita with such a drastically lower score?

We scan her credit report to see two dreaded figures: an "R" and a "5." Rita is shocked. What is it from? She had juggled everything so well, was diligent and organized! The vendor was a posh shoe store in town, and she opened a store card with them on a whim one day while making a purchase. She put two pairs of shoes on the card and promptly forgot about it! Due to an administrative error at the store, her phone number and address were entered incorrectly in the system. Letter after letter was returned undeliverable to the company, and the phone calls they made to Rita were answered by a Chinese restaurant.

Sound unbelievable? Amazingly, these types of situations occur all of the time! A friend of mine recently received a call from a collection agency regarding an account he closed almost 10 years earlier! As it turns out, there was a final balance on the account after it was closed. The company, the collection agency explained, could not reach him to reconcile the account, and it was sent to not one, but *four* collection agencies before he finally pulled his credit report and updated his contact information with Equifax. Here comes the really outrageous part: not only had he opened another account with this company since then, which was up to date with all of his current information, he *worked for the company for six of the nine years they were "trying" to track him down!*

Gary and Rita will benefit from a one- or a two-year term, depending on their debt repayment plan. They don't need a long time to repair their credit, but they may benefit from some extra time to pay off the rest of their debt and get on better footing for the future before they repurchase their house.

HELPING A TENANT IMPROVE THEIR CREDIT

Part of your job as a rent-to-own investor is offering suggestions to help your tenants improve their credit. I use the word "suggestion" because you ultimately cannot force them to do anything. If they're committed to credit repair, they will accept these suggestions and put them into action. In the end, though, you have no control; the tenant has to implement the changes. If you believe you have to monitor their credit repair program, you will drive yourself crazy and lose a lot of sleep. "But Mark," you may be saying, "if I'm unable to control their actions, they may not be able to buy the house at the end of the rental term!" True, but to ease your mind, remember this, and I will put it simply and brutally: if your tenant doesn't take the initiative and repair their credit, they forfeit their deposit and option credit, leaving you with money in your pocket. So, what are you worried about?

By the same token, you do need to take an interest in their credit repair. After all, the purchase of the house is your predetermined exit strategy! Do your part and make sure they know the steps to take, but after that it is entirely up to them whether they follow through.

To illustrate, let me tell you about a tenant I had in Alberta. He did a great job of improving his credit—so great, in fact, that three months before he was supposed to exercise the option to purchase, he applied and was approved for a brand-new truck! In doing so, he raised his total debt service ratio, and would no longer qualify to purchase the house at the end of the rental term. Between fantasies of shaking him until he came to his senses, I did the only thing that I could in the situation: I extended him to a 4.5-year term. This was the new time he needed to once again be able to qualify.

How can you safeguard against such a scenario? Connect your tenant with your credit repair specialist, who will work with the tenant to devise a plan they will execute throughout the rental term, the goal being that the tenants are mortgage-ready within the time frame of the rental term. Next, be involved. Review their credit bureau with them every three months. As they're coming to the end of their rental term, remind them that it's not the time to make any large purchases or change jobs—at least until they have closed on the property.

OBTAIN A SECURED CREDIT CARD

A secured credit card is also called a pre-paid credit card and works like this: instead of having credit extended to them, the client puts money on the card before they use it. They are not incurring debt because they have already paid the account before they spend, but by making regular payments and spending a small amount of the credit available each month, the tenant is establishing that they can make payments regularly. This will go a long way toward improving their credit score over time.

Suggest the tenant obtain a secured credit card, and once they do, they should set up a monthly bill to be paid from a company that reports to the credit bureau. You can determine which vendors the tenant uses who report to the credit bureau simply by looking on the report and seeing which companies are listed. This will provide a double benefit. Firstly, the tenant will establish a good payment history with the company, which will report the good payment to the credit bureau. Secondly, the company which issued the secured credit card will also be reporting a regular payment history to the credit bureau. This one action has a double impact on the credit report.

OBTAIN A REGULAR CREDIT CARD

If possible, have the client obtain a credit card. Even in today's economy, many companies will still issue a low balance card to someone with less than perfect credit. If they can obtain one, have them put two monthly payments on a card with a vendor which reports to the credit bureau. Suggest the tenant set up automatic payments to the credit card every month on a specific date *before* their due date. This way, they have charges going through each month, as well as payments, showing they are currently using credit (two trade lines) and establishing a fantastic payment history. They will also be spared having to pay interest on balances carried over.

SIGN UP FOR INTERNET BANKING

If they don't already use Internet banking through their financial institution, they should. Internet banking allows one to see finances at a quick glance and to set up automatic payments—a definite bonus for someone whose credit has taken a beating because their due dates simply slip their minds. These tools are available, and your tenants should be taking advantage of them to improve their situation.

NO NEW ACCOUNTS

Aside from the credit card or secured card we discussed above, make sure your tenants know not to open any new accounts or take any further credit. Doing so will affect their credit negatively in three ways: the hit on their credit report, the number of open accounts and the ratio of credit to available credit. New accounts will be counterproductive to the ultimate cause—getting the tenants mortgage-ready at the end of the rental term.

PROTECT THE BUREAU

Unless absolutely necessary, the tenant should not give their authorization to have a credit report pulled for any reason. Tell them to guard their social insurance number as though it were the Crown Jewels!

CONTINUE WORKING WITH THE CREDIT

To have poor payment history and then simply stop using credit altogether is a financial death sentence. In order to improve one's credit, it must be proved that the tenant can make regular payments for, at the very least, the minimum payment amount. Using credit is the only way to improve credit, so make sure your tenants know to keep using what they have—*in a responsible way!*

PAY DOWN REVOLVING ACCOUNTS

Revolving accounts, if you remember, are accounts where the amount of the monthly payment can vary, such as credit cards, and can be identified by the "R" rating on the credit bureau. Paying down revolving accounts to less than 50% shows restraint, helping the score section that looks at the applicant's ratio of used credit to available credit which, if you remember, is worth 30% of the entire credit score.

AUTOMATE ALL BILL PAYMENTS

To prevent potential future late payments (this is the big one, affecting 35% of the credit score!), advise your tenant to automate their payments for fixed accounts and set future payments for accounts that vary as soon as the bill arrives in the mail.

FIX ERRORS ON THE REPORT

Sometimes, creditors are slow to report accounts paid, or a report can have errors. Have the tenant contact the credit companies to have the errors fixed immediately to see quick improvements to their credit score. Advise them to keep all receipts when payments are made in case they are needed to remove the report from the bureau in the future.

NEGOTIATE LOWER PAYMENTS FOR ACCOUNTS IN COLLECTIONS

When a company writes off an account, the collection agency purchases it from the company and then attempts to get the money from the person owing. They are looking to recoup as much as possible. Therefore, they are usually willing to negotiate the final amount. A tenant can pay off their debts in collection a lot faster when they negotiate the price as low as possible.

WHEN THERE'S SOMETHING ON THE BUREAU THE APPLICANT DIDN'T DISCLOSE

Hopefully, you will never face this, but there is a possibility that you will find something on the credit report that the applicant didn't disclose in their application. Before you write off the applicant, first ask them about the item. Sometimes, things appear on the bureau that have long been paid off, and if the tenant claims this is the case, they should have some documentation proving it. This is usually referred to as a "discharge letter," but they may also have a receipt of payment that can prove the account has been settled. Often, an item on the bureau they did not disclose simply means the applicant did not know it was there in the first place, something that is easily rectified.

If the item is a significant amount and the potential tenant hasn't paid it, you have a decision to make—and most of the time you will need to bring your "gut feeling" about the tenant into the equation. Have they not disclosed the amount intentionally in an effort to deceive you? You will have to think long and hard about the situation, and depending on whether the TDS calculations still work with the undisclosed payment amount, you may have to walk away from the deal.

WALKING AWAY

From time to time, you will need to seriously consider walking away from an opportunity. Whether the numbers are bad or you have a negative feeling about the tenants, you should not go forward. There are plenty of opportunities with great tenants out there to be found, and it's better to pass up a questionable tenant to find a great tenant, than forge ahead with a deal and live to regret it.

If you are unsure whether your applicant can obtain financing at the end of the rental term, consult your mortgage broker, who can look at the tenant's credit situation and give you a realistic view.

THE INTENT TO OCCUPY AND INITIAL DEPOSIT

When an applicant has been approved and they're certain they're ready to move forward, it's a good idea to get a little money from them right off the bat to ensure they are serious. Usually, the amount is $500, which will be a portion of their total deposit, and it is non-refundable if the applicant backs out. How much you ask for up front is entirely up to you, but make sure it's enough to give you the confidence that the tenant is serious. Some refer to this initial deposit as an "application fee." Just like the amount, whatever you call it or how you explain it is up to you.

There are two reasons getting a portion of the money up front is a good idea. First, the tenant putting money forward shows they are serious about the process. If they're serious about renting to own a property, they probably have their deposit already and, with the appropriate documentation, will not have a problem using a small portion of their deposit to get the ball rolling. The second reason to have the tenant put money down is to quantify the process. Studies have shown that when there is a price on something, people value it more. By putting a dollar amount on the application process, the applicant will be less inclined to walk away and leave you with nothing for your time and effort. But how does the tenant know their initial deposit is going toward their final deposit, and what gives you the right, contractually, to keep the $500 if the client walks away? The answer is: the intent to occupy.

An intent to occupy is an agreement the soon-to-be tenant should sign, stating they do intend to lease the property. Without this, having the tenant select a house has the possibility to be a gigantic waste of time. The intent to occupy is a short contract that should be signed before the home search begins. The wording of the intent to occupy is up to you, but it absolutely must contain specific points in order to protect your interests. Somewhere within the document, it must state the applicant's name and the sum of money you are to receive from them, and your name as one accepting the funds. The applicant should have a period of time in which they can cancel the contract and receive their initial deposit back (usually 48 hours after signing), and then after that period the money is non-refundable. It should also state that when the rent-to-own deal is complete, the initial deposit will go toward the deposit. Here is a sample of the intent to occupy that I use:

INTENT TO OCCUPY

Received from _____ hereinafter referred to as the "Applicant(s)," the sum of _____ ($_____), which upon acceptance of this application by _____, as an application fee. The applicant has the right within 48 hours to cancel this application; where the deposit received shall be fully refunded. After this period, this application fee is deemed non-refundable. Upon successful completion of the rent-to-own transaction, the application fee will be credited toward the deposit of the rent-to-own agreement.

_____   _____   _____
Signature of Applicant   Date   Signature of Co-Applicant
Date

_____   _____   _____
Address   Signature of Witness   Date

_____

IN REVIEW

Assess the applicant's credit bureau and, if applicable, determine when bankruptcy will be discharged. Offer suggestions to help improve their credit and connect the tenant with a credit repair specialist. Have the client send the initial deposit and intent to occupy to get the ball rolling.

CHAPTER 11
The Financial Analysis Spreadsheet

Now you have your ideal tenant, they have put up a bit of their deposit to show you they mean business and you have a signed intent to occupy contract. It is time to move forward and determine monthly lease payments, option credit and appreciation rate, which will determine the final buy-out price.

The first step is to find or create a sound financial analysis spreadsheet. This will allow you to quickly run the numbers, assess the deal and decide whether to move forward. A good financial spreadsheet includes the purchase price of the house (or a pre-approved amount, if the tenant has not yet found their ideal home), the deposit the tenant is putting down, legal costs, land transfer taxes (if applicable) and an appreciation rate based on the term you determine the tenant needs, and location. Naturally, since your tenant does not yet have a house, you will be running preliminary numbers based on either the purchase price they have in mind or for which they have been approved.

The spreadsheet should readily calculate figures for you, including final purchase price, lease payments, option credit and, of course, return on investment. With your handy financial analysis spreadsheet, you should be able to plug in the numbers for the deal and have the totals automatically calculate. It should also allow you to change the calculation amounts so you can find the best deal for both you and the tenant. For instance, based on TDS and the approximate lease payment the tenant has told me they would like to pay, I could juggle the lease payment calculation between .008 and .0095 and, in seconds, be able to see my return on investment for each calculation. You can find the one I use at www.theversatileinvestor.com, complete with the calculation cells in working order, but you may also create your own spreadsheet.

Let's return to our hypothetical tenants, Jonathan and Cindy and Gary and Rita. Now that they have all decided to move forward with the rent-to-own process, there are a number of things we need to do to make sure we are protecting our interests as well as making it a win/win for everyone involved.

THE PURCHASE PRICE

There are a few things we need to know ahead of time. The first is the purchase price of the house the tenants would like to buy, or, if the tenant does not yet have a house picked out and you are strictly juggling the numbers, you can use the purchase price for which they have already been approved. Jonathan and Cindy have been "pre-approved" for $400,000. Gary and Rita have qualified for $550,000 to rent to own their current house.

THE LEASE RATE

The second item you will need for your spreadsheet is the rate at which their lease will be calculated. As demonstrated in our example with both Jonathan and Cindy and Rita and Gary, I use a calculation of between .008 and .0095 of the purchase price, depending on many factors such as the city in which they want to live, economic conditions and the amount the applicants feel comfortable spending each month.

THE DEPOSIT

Third, you need to know how much of a deposit the applicant will put forward. The deposit will be held toward their down payment at the end of the rental term to be added to their 20% option credit. I like to take anywhere between 2 and 5% for a deposit, but you may want to request more from the tenant. The deposit is important for a number of reasons, particularly that the amount the tenant puts down will ultimately secure your investment. If one tenant puts down $2,000 and the other $21,000, which tenant is less likely to walk away from the deal, not purchasing the house in the end or, even worse, staging a midnight move? It's a lot more difficult for someone to walk away from a large chunk of money because they have more "skin in the game," so to speak. Use a 2% deposit as a bare minimum, and negotiate with the tenant to get a larger amount. Try asking them what they can put down rather than immediately telling them what they *should* put down. Often, those who are serious about doing a rent to own will offer up a larger deposit than you would have asked for. If you have to give the tenant a number, always begin with a higher amount, and work down if you need to. If you ask for 5%, you will probably get it. In certain situations where you want added security, you may ask for a deposit in excess of 5%, but this is rare and should only be done if you want to secure your investment further. Keep your eye out for quality applicants who make good money and have long job tenure, and you will not have to take such steps for security.

It's also a good idea to ask for a fraction of the deposit up front as a sign of good faith. I usually request $500 from a serious tenant to get the ball rolling. This is non-refundable if the applicant decides to back out. Your time is worth far more than that, of course, but the minute you assign a dollar value to something, you quickly determine whether the person is serious.

When discussing a deposit, begin by asking the tenant how much they can put down. Often in the case of people with stable, adequate income but poor credit, the tenant already has a number in mind. You don't want to ask them for the bare minimum of 2% if they're able to give 10%! Based on their reply, gauge how their deposit will affect the deal using your financial analysis spreadsheet. If you're feeling unsure about a particular deal, you may want to ask for a larger deposit to secure your investment.

In following with our practice of learning from the mistakes of others, I would like to tell you about an investor friend of mine who learned a hard lesson, indeed. He had a number of rent-to-own properties at this point, and was embarking on his thirteenth deal. His tenants qualified, had chosen their house and everything was shaping up well, but they didn't have enough money for their deposit. Being a nice guy, my investor friend decided he would still take them as tenants, and offer them a plan to pay their deposit over the first few months of their rental period. Naturally, the tenants were ecstatic, and a payment plan was devised. However, by the time the third month rolled around, he still had not seen any of the deposit payments they promised! A few more months passed, and it became clear to my friend that they weren't going to pay. At this point, not only was he out the deposit, he also had not received their rent! When he confronted them about it, they confessed they didn't have the money and had been overly ambitious in foreseeing their ability to pay the deposit. My friend had to evict the tenants and start over with a traditional rent to own, faced with the difficult task of finding new tenants who would love the house the others had chosen. He was still on the hook for the mortgage during the months no one occupied the house, and the stress he endured was enough to make even the most seasoned investor's head spin. Learn from my friend's mistake. Always get the deposit up front, and follow the procedures I have outlined.

If a tenant doesn't have the minimum 2% deposit but are clearly motivated to be home owners through rent to own, I will give them the option to pay their deposit in instalments—*before* they choose or occupy a house. I then work out a plan with the tenants to pay the deposit over time, since I find that without a plan, people tend to do nothing. In the past, I have accepted $500 a month from such tenants, and put their money in trust until they build a complete deposit and we could proceed. A tenant without a deposit is not a lost cause, but they won't get their foot in the door of a property until they come up with the funds.

Jonathan and Cindy inform us they are able to put down $12,000, which is a deposit of 3%. We ask if they could possibly do $15,000. After talking it over, Jonathan and Cindy decide they can squeeze the extra $3,000 from their regular income. Great!

Gary and Rita are using the equity already in their home toward their down payment, and that works well for us. In addition, they are able to scrape together 2%, making their deposit $11,000.

LAND TRANSFER TAX

Land Transfer Tax is something you will most likely need to take into account when analyzing a deal. Most provinces in Canada have such a tax, and the rate varies. There are many online land transfer tax calculators one can access for free, which makes running the numbers of a potential deal much easier. Search for "land transfer tax calculator" for Canada and the results should give you a number of sites where you simply punch in the purchase price and designate the province in which the property is located. You will receive the land transfer tax amount instantly! Keep in mind that Alberta, Saskatchewan and rural Nova Scotia do not have LTT. The other provinces use a tiered system, and the rate you pay varies depending on the purchase price of the house.

Fortunately for Tim, Jonathan and Cindy live in Alberta, so he doesn't have to worry about land transfer tax. When purchasing Gary and Rita's house, however, Tim will need to calculate the land transfer tax based on the Ontario rate, which, for a purchase price of more than $400,000, is 1.5% of the total property value. When Tim and his joint-venture partner purchase Gary and Rita's house, they will be paying $6,000.

After factoring in the purchase price, deposit, the lease rate, land transfer tax and finding a lease payment with which Jonathan and Cindy feel comfortable, we are only steps away from determining our final return on investment.

If you are proficient in Microsoft Excel or similar programs, you can put together your own financial analysis spreadsheet with pre-calculating cells. This is particularly handy when you're trying to analyze deals on the fly, say on your laptop or PDA. My financial analysis spreadsheet calculates based on both 90 and 80% financing, and includes a mortgage calculation spreadsheet for both scenarios. For those who don't want to create their own spreadsheets, I have posted mine for your use at www.theversatileinvestor.com.

Now that you've used your financial analysis spreadsheet to run preliminary numbers for a potential deal based on a pre-approved purchase price or a house the tenants have in mind, you can return to the spreadsheet after you know the actual price of the house. Plug in the new numbers for a precise monthly lease payment, option credit, final buy-out price and, of course, your monthly cash flow and return on investment.

Let's take a look at how Gary and Rita and Jonathan and Cindy's financial analysis spreadsheets looked after Tim ran the numbers:

Financial Analysis - Jonathan and Cindy
3 Year Term
Edmonton

	%	Monthly Figures	Actual Figures
Purchase Price			$400,000
Financing Information			
1st Mortgage	80%		$320,000
Total Mortgage			$320,000

	%	Monthly Figures	Actual Figures
Investment			
Down Payment	20%		$80,000
Land Transfer Tax			$0
Legal Costs			$1,500
Disbursements (GST + PST)			$0
Less: Security Deposit			
(from Lessee)			($8,000)
Total Investment	18.38%		$73,500
Profit from Sale/Transfer			
Sale/Transfer Price			$476,406
Add: Exercise of Option Fee			$3,400
Less: Remaining 1st Mortgage			($320,000)
Less: Legal Cost to Discharge			($350)
Less: Initial Investment			($73,500)
Less: Security Deposit			
(from Lessee)			($8,000)
Less: Monthly Credits			
to Lessee	$680	36	($24,480)
Total Profit from Sale/Transfer			$53,476
Gain From Monthly Cashflow			
Lease Payments	$3,400	$122,400	
Less: Debt Service—			
1st Mortgage	4.50%	($1,506)	($54,222)
Less: Property Tax		($305)	($10,980)
Less: Insurance		(65.00)	($2,340)
Less: Maintenance Fee		0	$0
Total Profit from Cashflow		$1,524	$54,858
Net Profit			$108,334
Return on Investment (Per Annum)			49%

Financial Analysis - Gary and Rita
2 Year Term
Markham

	%	Monthly Figures	Actual Figures
Purchase Price			$550,000
Financing Information			
1st Mortgage	80%		$440,000
Total Mortgage			$440,000
Investment			
Down Payment	20%		$110,000
Land Transfer Tax			$7,475
Legal Costs			$1,148
Disbursements (GST + PST)			$0
Less: Security Deposit			
(from Lessee)			($11,000)
Total Investment	19.57%		$107,623
Profit from Sale/Transfer			
Sale/Transfer Price			$617,980
Less: Remaining			
1st Mortgage			($440,000)
Less: Legal Cost to Discharge			($350)
Less: Initial Investment			($107,623)
Less: Security Deposit			
(from Lessee)			($11,000)
Less: Monthly Credits			
to Lessee	$825	24	($19,800)
Total Profit from Sale/Transfer			$39,208
Gain From Monthly Cashflow			
Lease Payments		$4,125	$99,000
Less: Debt Service—			
1st Mortgage 4.50%		($2,071)	($49,704)
Less: Property Tax		($385)	($9,239)
Less: Insurance		(65.00)	($1,560)
Less: Maintenance Fee		0	$0
Total Profit from Cashflow		$1,604	$38,497
Net Profit			$77,705
Return on Investment (Per Annum)			36%

IN REVIEW

A good financial analysis spreadsheet will be invaluable. Use the one I have provided at www.theversatileinvestor.com or create your own.

PART 3

FINDING AND PURCHASING THE PROPERTY

CHAPTER 12

The Tenant Finds a Home

We have successfully found a tenant for our tenant-first rent-to-own strategy. So, the next logical step is to find them somewhere to live! Keep in mind that this part of the process is unnecessary if the tenant already owns their house, like Gary and Rita. But in a refinancing situation such as Gary and Rita's rent to own, I always insist upon an appraisal ahead of time.

When your tenant is looking for a house, you will rely heavily on the realtor in your immediate networking sphere. Here is where this plan differs from most rent-to-own strategies. Usually the investor finds the property first, but to give the tenant a choice of their house and prevent weeks of searching for a tenant who wants to own the house the investor has purchased, we find the tenant first and then search for the property. This is another example of when your network will truly serve you.

As soon as the tenant submits their $500 and the signed intent to occupy document, I set them up with a realtor in their area. I prefer to use a realtor I know for a number of different reasons. First, my realtor will already be aware of the rent-to-own program, and know that ultimately it will be me purchasing the house, not the tenants. Despite this, my realtor will take the tenant under his or her wing and treat them as though they are their client, showing them suitable houses. The realtors I use know the good and bad areas, and are more interested in getting the tenant a good home while protecting my interests than simply closing a deal. I trust the realtors in my immediate sphere to do this, and you can't put a price on that!

What if you don't have a realtor? Of course, my advice is that you should do everything in your power to find one. Call other investors for recommendations, for realtors they know, like and trust. If the tenant chooses their own realtor, it's a good idea to touch base with the agent over the phone or perhaps in person over lunch, and discuss the tenant-first rent-to-own strategy with them. It's important the realtor understand what the tenant-first strategy means for the tenants, for you as the investor, and for them.

For the most part, you will allow the tenant to choose the house they like. However, try to steer them toward single-family homes because they're better investments for you. There are more buyers for these types of homes, compared to duplexes or multi-family units, and therefore will be easier to resell if you ever need to.

The situation might arise that the tenant already has an affiliation with a realtor, perhaps someone they were using before they became aware they couldn't obtain financing. As with most mortgage professionals, realtors work very hard for their money, and they don't get paid until a deal closes. Chances are, if the tenants have been dealing with a realtor already, that realtor has invested a lot of time in finding them a property, and it's only fair they get their commission for the deal. Again, it is important to sit down with this realtor face to face or over the phone to explain the situation, so they clearly understand the process. Learning that their client—to this point a would-be buyer but now a "tenant"—with whom they have invested numerous hours is not going to be the one buying the house can threaten some realtors. Once they understand exactly what it means for them, they usually become enthusiastic about the process. After all, without the rent-to-own option, the deal would have fallen apart and they would have received nothing. At least with you purchasing the house instead of the tenants, they still have the potential to close the deal and make their commission, and that is usually enough to make most realtors happy.

And we want our realtors to be happy! A realtor has the power to make things very difficult when you're trying to close a deal, and this is the number one reason I like to use a realtor I know and trust. In fact, a difficult realtor can even prevent the deal from going through, or worse, talk your tenants out of doing a rent to own.

Unfortunately, I do have experience with this exact situation. A young couple wanted to purchase their first house, and were excited about the option I offered. The realtor they had been dealing with was less enthusiastic, though, and despite numerous conversations with her explaining how she would benefit, the realtor was convinced there was an angle she was missing—a way that she would somehow get the short end of the stick. No matter how I tried to explain the benefits to her, she wouldn't listen, so we decided not to work together. I contacted a realtor in my network and connected them with the couple who wanted to buy. Sadly, the realtor had already spoken with the tenants and fed them some misinformation about the program, which was enough to plant the seed of doubt in their minds. The next thing I knew, my enthusiastic young tenants turned their back on their dream home, and home ownership altogether, and decided to continue renting until their credit was good enough to obtain a mortgage. I respected their decision and left the door open for them to return at any time, but the damage had been done. All the time I spent on the deal was for nothing, and in the end, the tenants were the ones who suffered the most due to some misinformation from a realtor with preconceived notions.

The moral of the story is this: if you cannot use a realtor from your sphere that you trust, make sure you sit down with an agent and give them all the information so they truly understand how they will benefit. Further, if the telephone conversation or lunch meeting goes well, have them send you qualified tenants in the future! With the tenant-first rent-to-own strategy, an investor can never have too many allies.

THE HOUSE HUNT

Once the tenant is connected with a realtor and you're sure they will protect the interests of both you and your tenants, it's time to begin the search for a house! This is one of the best parts of the tenant-first rent-to-own program. It's exciting for the tenant, as they have essentially been given an amount they can spend and have been told to go pick out a house. It's like going "shopping" for their dream home.

The tenant must let the realtor know specifically what they are looking for. Do they want a back yard? How many bedrooms and bathrooms do they need? Would their ideal home be in a specific neighborhood? Close to schools or churches? As far away from the in-laws as possible?

Once the realtor and tenant have discussed the type of house and nearby amenities they desire, the realtor can begin showing the tenants some properties. For the first time since this process began, you as the investor get to sit back and relax a little. There is not much you can do to expedite things, so you can take a little holiday, catch up on your yard work, or, if you are so ambitious, start searching for more potential tenants for your next deal.

Hopefully, not too long after the search began, your phone will ring and either the tenant or the realtor will tell you they have found the perfect house! Time to stop slacking, it's back to work! There are a number of things that need to be arranged, for which you can try out your new network of professionals.

THE HOME INSPECTION

Regardless of what the seller, tenant or realtor says, get a home inspection. You have been networking for the past few months, so at this point you should already have a good home inspector lined up. If you haven't yet found one, call other real estate investors for referrals or consult your local Yellow Pages (or web equivalent) and start shopping. The realtor you use should have some referrals for home inspectors as well.

It's the tenant's responsibility to pay for the home inspection. It's in their best interests to know the condition of the house, the issues that need to be re-solved immediately and any looming problems that will need to be addressed in the future. Discuss this with the tenant ahead of time so they're not surprised when the home inspector delivers their invoice.

If you can, be present for the home inspection, and get involved. Ask the inspector to explain things they identify, and inquire as to when the issues need to be fixed. If you can't attend, request an online copy of the inspection. The tenants should also be present; it is, for all intents and purposes, their house, and they need to be involved as part of the responsibility of home ownership.

Chances are the home inspection will go well and the property will receive rave reviews. But what if the inspection cites issues such as cracked founda-tion, plumbing or electrical issues or problems with the roof? Yes, this kind of review is enough to get an investor's heart racing, but there is good news on the bad home inspection front. You, the investor, are not responsible for the cost of the repairs. It is the tenant's responsibility to take care of any problems with the house before you, the investor, purchase the property. This is written into the home repairs agreement, and if the tenant has read their contract and you have discussed the details with them properly, they will already be aware of their responsibilities.

For major issues, you can request that the seller pay for the repairs before you purchase the house. Discuss the issues with the tenant and give them the choice to repair the problems or search for another home. If the tenant decides to repair any issues, ask for details from the contractors or any other professionals they'll need to hire. This is part of your due diligence. It's not enough to take the tenant's word for it that the issues have been resolved. You must do everything in your power to protect your investment, and that includes verifying that the tenants have upheld their end of the bargain, in this case repairing things that need to be fixed. In your repairs contract, make sure you have outlined a deadline for when each repair must be made. A sample of such a contract can be found in Chapter 13.

If the tenant decides to walk away, that's okay too. The process begins again with the realtor and tenant, and you get to take another mini holiday! When the phone rings again, you'll have your home inspector ready to go.

Performing your own at-a-glance home inspection

If you perform a preliminary viewing of the property before the official home inspection, there are certain things to watch for. These are real techniques I use each and every time I view a property with a tenant in the interest of saving time and, of course, saving the tenant the cost of a home inspection.

- Turn off all of the lights in the house and then take a photo with a digital camera. Make sure the flash is on, and photograph the entire ceiling around the room. If there are watermarks on the ceiling, they will show up in the picture. Water damage is not always easy to see, and this is a great quick and easy way to check for leaks in the roof or second-floor plumbing.

- Check for knob and tube wiring, which can still be found in the basement of many older houses. Knob and tube wiring can be identified by wire running between ceramic cylinders. If a home still has this type of wiring, you will need to have the electrical redone—not a cheap job! Knob and tube wiring is unreliable and flimsy, not to mention a fire hazard—something sure to send an insurance company running in the opposite direction!

- Check the age of the furnace. The average furnace has a life of 20 to 25 years, but that's only if it has been properly maintained. If it's older than 20 years, it will probably need to be replaced immediately or shortly after the house is purchased.

- If you're viewing the house in the winter, you can use the cold temperatures to help you look for faults in construction. Icicles may be picturesque, but they can also tell you something very important about the house. If you see any icicles, even small ones, this usually indicates heat loss coming from the attic due to inadequate insulation. If you view a house in the summer, ask the sellers if they have icicles, or better yet, ask the neighbors.

- Invest in a thermal imager. These handy little devices cost about $60 and are available at stores such as Canadian Tire. A thermal imager detects heat or temperature in objects, and works much like a camera or camcorder, only instead of taking a photo of what's visible to the naked eye, essentially it takes a picture of levels of heat. The image you see would show heat in yellow or white, and cooler temperatures in blue. Thermal imagers have many uses when looking at a potential investment property, such as revealing mould, bug infestations and water damage. When looking at a fuse box and other electrical points, a thermal imager can show faults in a fuse block. It can show places where water is seeping into the house, a lack of insulation in the wall, a hot breaker, air leaks, energy voids, moisture and much more.

- Insist the seller be present at the time of the viewing. Meeting the seller will allow you to ask questions about the things you see, and you'll be able to gauge their reaction to your questions to help determine their reasons for selling. If the house is a money pit that's only going to cause stress and heartache, let them unload their "problem" on someone else!

IN REVIEW

Connect the tenant with a realtor you trust and who knows the area well. Once a house has been identified, a house inspection must be performed. You can also view the house before the official inspection to identify any obvious problems.

CHAPTER 13

Financing the Rental Property

In a case where the tenant already owns their home, such as Gary and Rita, you can skip the house hunt and move directly to the purchase. This is the time when we call in the next "batter" on our team—the mortgage broker. Remember, the mortgage broker's job is to search lenders and find you the best deal, just as a travel agent would shop the airlines on your behalf to get you a great rate on your holiday.

This step shouldn't take long, and your broker will walk you through the entire process if you're not already familiar with it. You will need to fill out a mortgage application and disclose all sorts of highly personal information, so you want to make sure you have a good broker. As we talked about in the section on building your network, your mortgage broker should be familiar with real estate investing or, even better, an investor themselves. This will make the entire process a lot smoother; when an investor purchases a property for the purpose of renting or leasing it in any capacity, a lender needs to see proof, without which the financing could be declined.

SUBMITTING AN OFFER TO PURCHASE

The tenant has found the house of their dreams! It's within the amount for which they are pre-approved and has most of what they're looking for. It's now time to submit an offer, known as the offer to purchase or an agreement of purchase and sale.

The agreement of purchase and sale is a very specific document that outlines the conditions and terms for the buyer (in this case, you, the investor) and the seller. The offer you put in will usually be lower than the asking price because, of course, you want to get the best deal possible. Sometimes the first offer is accepted, but often a process of negotiation ensues. A good realtor will determine the seller's motivation ahead of time, and will have a pretty clear idea of what the final purchase price will be in the end.

Your realtor will be the middle man (or woman) and will liaise with the seller's agent, who may make a counter offer. This back and forth negotiation of the purchase price will continue until the seller accepts your offer. Sometimes, it's a one-step process, and other times it can go on for a while and be influenced largely by the seller's motivation. If they want to "unload" the house, they may accept your offer faster than if they have a strong emotional attachment to the property or have a specific price they want to receive. Most of the time, a seller's asking price is "high-balled," meaning that in anticipation of negotiation, they price it higher, expecting to receive a lower offer than the listed price. You may counter with a "low-balled" price, in anticipation of the seller's counter price. If there is another party bidding on the property, the seller may accept the other offer instead of yours. Ask your realtor to find out if there is any other negotiation in progress. Once the seller accepts your offer, the agreement of purchase and sale becomes a legally binding document, outlining the obligations of you and the seller to complete the deal. It's your responsibility to ensure you understand the intricacies of the agreement before you sign it and bind yourself to the stipulations therein. The agreement of purchase and sale will outline inclusions such as appliances and draperies (known as chattels) that are to be included in the sale price. Most agreements are standardized, so the realtor will not have to amend the document too much. Anything you want included in the purchase should be specified in advance, so it can be included in the document. The agreement will also set out any conditions that must be satisfied prior to closing. The closing date itself, usually 30 to 60 days after the date of the agreement (but possibly as long as 90 days, depending on when the tenants want to move in) will be specified within the contract.

Drafting and understanding all of the terms in an agreement of purchase and sale is a book in itself, which is yet another reason you need a quality realtor in your corner. As an investor, you do not need to burden yourself with these details. Having said that, ensure you still perform your due diligence by clarifying anything in the contract you don't understand or that you want included. Most agreements of purchase and sale carry conditions that need to be carried out for the contract to be valid, such as an appraisal of the property, a home inspection and financing. Once these conditions have been met, the conditions are removed and the agreement of purchase and sale, now the offer to purchase, becomes final.

OBTAINING FINANCING

Even if you have been pre-approved, it's not a guarantee that you will receive financing—something that is a shock to most "pre-approved" investors.

Your mortgage broker should begin the search for financing when the offer to purchase is in the "conditional" phase, meaning before the conditions are removed. Of course, since most offers carry a condition for financing, conditions are usually not removed until the financing has been arranged, so this step will occur before the offer to purchase becomes final.

You will need to provide the mortgage broker with the offer to purchase and the property listing, so they can properly begin the financing search.

The lender will also have some conditions that will need to be met, called "financing conditions." These could include an appraisal by a bank-approved appraisal company, a survey and proof of title insurance.

A lender will require a down payment from you, usually between 10 and 20%. Anything less than a 20% down payment will usually require mortgage loan insurance.

There are a number of different types of mortgages, and to get into each type would turn this book into something that resembles the Encyclopaedia Britannica. Your mortgage broker can discuss the different options available for your financing in detail, and answer any questions you may have.

JONATHAN AND CINDY PURCHASE THEIR HOUSE

Now that they're approved and Jonathan and Cindy have given our friend Tim $500 and a signed intent to occupy agreement, Tim flips through his networking file to find them a realtor in the area who he knows and likes, and who understands the tenant-first rent-to-own strategy. Good thing he went to all of those networking events, because his first choice is out of town, off on a two-month cruise through the Bahamas. Muttering something about how it must be a rough life for his realtor, he flips to the next contact in his system and gives

Julie a call. Julie is a realtor in Alberta who knows the province-specific rules, and Tim is pleased to find she's going to be available between now and the time the deal with Jonathan and Cindy is set up.

While he has Julie on the phone, Tim asks her if she knows any good realtors in the Greater Toronto Area. He doesn't have anyone for the area yet that he's crazy about, and besides, getting more referrals from realtors for qualified tenants is always a good thing (see how that works?). Yes, Julie says, as a matter of fact, her cousin is a realtor in the area, and she offers to cyber-introduce them the following day.

After hanging up with Julie, Tim calls Jonathan and Cindy and gives them Julie's contact information. Tim learns, via email, that they have set up a time to go house hunting the following day, and that based on the things they're looking for in a house, Julie is confident the search won't take long.

Shortly after, Tim receives the cyber intro via email from Julie. The email contains Julie's cousin Max's contact information. On a bit of a real-estate-investing-success high, Tim immediately picks up the phone and calls Max, who already has some potential tenants in mind from his previous client list. Within minutes of speaking with Max, Tim hangs up the phone once again, props his heels up on the edge of his desk and crosses his hands behind his head. "This is not difficult," he thinks with a sigh. "Why didn't I do this ages ago?" And with a silly grin sneaking out of the corner of his mouth, Tim drifts off to sleep, taking a much-deserved afternoon nap.

One week after his initial contact with Julie, Jonathan and Cindy's realtor, Tim receives a call from a very enthusiastic Cindy. She won the coin toss over who would call Tim with the good news: they have found a house and want to put in an offer! "Back to work," Tim thinks as he dials Julie and gets ready for the process of buying the house of Jonathan and Cindy's dreams.

Julie draws up an offer to purchase, and submits it to the seller. By dinner time, the phone calls are flying back and forth as Julie negotiates the lowest price possible with the seller's realtor. Tim's cell phone is ringing at the dinner table, but for once his wife does not scold him for it. She is ecstatic that Tim's new real estate endeavor is actually working out (and seemingly better than the last one!), and besides, he is clearly enjoying his new role in the fast lane of real estate investing. How could she rain on his parade?

By the time the custard appears on the dinner table, Julie and Tim have an accepted offer. Tim will pay $385,000 for the house, $15,000 less than the amount for which they were originally approved! With custard sliding down his chin, Tim tells his family the good news, wipes his mouth and then sets out to call Jonathan and Cindy to congratulate them—they are going to be home owners!

Tim's next step with Jonathan and Cindy is to obtain financing, and for this he calls his mortgage broker, Chris. Chris is licensed in Alberta even though he lives in Ontario, so he's a good resource for Tim, as he will be able to arrange most of his financing, regardless of where Tim decides to invest. "Leave it to me," Chris tells him, and once again, Tim hangs up the phone, leans back in his chair and settles in for a nap. Little does he know this time that one of the wheels of his office chair is balanced on a rogue baby toy, and he falls out of the chair onto the floor. No comfortable nap for Tim tonight! Instead, he heads off to help his wife with the dishes.

PART 4

THE PAPERWORK

CHAPTER 14

Various Agreements and Option to Purchase

With any real estate deal, one of the most important things to get right is the paperwork. With a rent to own, there are a few additional documents you must have drawn up to obtain financing, make the terms of the rent-to-own official and protect your investment throughout the rental period.

THE LEASE AGREEMENT

There are three documents you will need to have your tenants sign, the first of which is the lease agreement. This is a document you may need to obtain financing to prove to lenders that you have an agreement with a tenant already in place. There are many lease agreements out there, and an Internet search for "sample lease agreements" will produce a number of standard agreements you can use. The lease agreement must cover the lease term with the end date of the agreement and the monthly payment. As always, you can obtain your own lease agreement online or from someone in your network, but I have included the following sample.

Lease Contract

Received from: _____ (tenant), hereinafter referred to as the "Occupant," the sum of
$_____ (deposit) which, upon acceptance of this Lease by the
Owner of the premises, hereinafter referred to as Owner, shall be applied as follows:

In the event that this agreement is not accepted by the Owner or his
authorized agent, within 7 days, the total deposit received shall be refunded. Occupant hereby offers to lease from the Owner the premises
situated in the
City of _____, in the Province of _____, located at
_____ (address) upon the following TERMS and
CONDITIONS.

TERM: The term hereof shall commence on _____
(the lease start date) and continue for a period of ____ (the number of
months in the rental agreement) months thereafter.

RENT: Rent shall be $ _____ per month, as noted above, payable
in advance, *before* the FIRST (1ˢᵗ) day of each calendar month to Owner at the address below, or such other places as may be designated by
Owner from time to time. In the event rent is not paid, Occupant is in
Default under the Lease and Option. The Option may be deemed null
and void, and the Monthly Credits accumulated are forfeited as liquidated damages and not as a penalty, in accordance with DEFAULT
provisions below.

UTILITIES: Occupant shall be responsible for the payment of all
utilities and services.

USE: The premises shall be used as residence with no more than
_____ adults and _____ children, and for no other purpose, without
the prior written consent of the Owner.

LAWS & REGULATIONS: Occupant shall comply with all laws, regulations and requirements of all municipal, provincial and federal authorities now in force, or which may hereafter be in force, pertaining to the use of the premises.

ASSIGNMENT & SUBLETTING: Occupant shall not assign this agreement or sublet any portion of the premises without the prior written consent of the Owner which may not be unreasonably withheld.

MAINTENANCE & REPAIRS OR ALTERATIONS: Occupant acknowledges that the premises are in good order and repair, unless otherwise indicated herein. Owner may at any time give Occupant a written inventory of furniture and furnishings on the premises and Occupant shall be deemed to have possession of all said furniture and furnishings in good condition and repair, unless he objects thereto in writing within 5 (FIVE) days after receipts of such inventory. Occupant shall water and maintain any surrounding grounds, including lawns and shrubbery, and keep the same clear of rubbish or weeds, if such grounds are part of the premises and are exclusively for the use of the Occupant. Occupant shall, at his own expense, maintain the premises in a clean and sanitary manner including all equipment, appliances, furniture and furnishings therein and shall Surrender the same at termination hereof, in good condition as received, normal wear and tear excepted.

Occupant may paint, paper or otherwise redecorate or make alterations to the premises WITH the prior written consent of the Owner. Should Occupant leave or not exercise the option, or this agreement is cancelled for any reason, there will be no credit or consideration returned for repairs, alterations or decorations.
ALL costs to be paid 100% by the Occupant.

ENTRY & INSPECTION: Occupant shall permit Owner or Owner's agents to enter the premises at reasonable times and upon reasonable notice for the purpose of inspecting the premises or showing the same to prospective Occupants or purchasers, or for making necessary repairs.

INDEMNIFICATION and INSURANCE: Owner shall not be liable for any damage or injury to Occupant, or any other person, or to any property, occurring on the premises, or any part thereof, or in common areas thereof, and Occupant agrees to hold Owner harmless from any claims for damages no matter how caused. Occupant must maintain owner approved "Occupant Insurance," and provide ongoing verification copies to Owner.

POSSESSION: If Owner is unable to deliver possession of the premises at the commencement hereof, Owner shall not be liable for any damage caused thereby, nor shall this agreement be voided or voidable but Occupant shall not be liable for any rent until possession is delivered.

DEFAULT: The failure by Occupant to pay rent when due, or perform any term hereof, shall, at the option of the Owner, terminate all rights of Occupant hereunder. In the event that Occupant shall be absent from the premises for a period of 5 (FIVE) consecutive days, while in default, Occupant shall at the option of the Owner, be deemed to have abandoned the premises and any property left on the premises shall be considered abandoned and may be disposed of by the Owner in any manner allowed by law. In the event that Owner reasonably believes that such abandoned property has no value, it may be discarded. All property on the premises is hereby subject to a lien in favor of Owner, for payment of all sums due hereunder, to the maximum extent allowed by law.

Recover of the premises by Owner shall not relieve Occupant of any obligation hereunder, and Owner may lease the premises to others upon such terms and conditions he deems proper, and recover from

Occupant sums due hereunder, less any consideration received from others for the use of the premises, for the remaining term hereof, after paying expenses.

SECURITY: The security deposit set forth above, if any, shall secure the performance of Occupant's obligations hereunder, Owner may, but shall not be obligated to apply all or portions of said deposit on account of Occupant's obligations hereunder. Any balance remaining upon termination shall be returned to Occupant.

DEPOSIT FUNDS: Any returnable deposits shall be refunded in 10 (TEN) days from date possession is delivered to Owner or his authorized agent.

LEGAL FEES: In the event that Owner shall prevail in any legal action brought by either party to enforce the terms hereof or relating to the demised premises, Owner shall be entitled to all costs incurred in connection with such action, including legal fees on a solicitor and his own client, full indemnity basis. The Owner is entitled to recover an allowance for HIS time and effort expended with respect to any default recovery proceedings at $50.00 per hour. Such allowance to be reasonable and comparable with what the Owner would pay to a third party for a similar time and effort.

WAIVER: No failure of Owner to enforce any term hereof shall be deemed a waiver, nor shall any acceptance of a partial payment of rent be deemed a waiver of Owner's right to full amount of refund.

NOTICES: Any notice which either party may or is required to give, may be given by mailing the same postage prepaid, to Occupant at the premises or to Owner at the address shown below or at such other places as may be designated by the parties from time to time.

HEIRS, ASSIGNS, & SUCCESSORS: This lease is binding upon and inures to the benefit of the heirs, assigns and successors in interest to the parties.

TIME: Time is of the essence in this agreement.

ACCEPTANCE: The undersigned Owner accepts the foregoing offer and acknowledges receipt of a copy hereof.
The undersigned Occupant hereby acknowledges receipt of a copy hereof.

_____   _____
Signature of Witness   *Date*   *Signature of Occupant*   *Date*

_____   _____
Address   *Signature of Occupant*   *Date*

_____   _____
Phone   *Signature of Owner*   *Date*

_____   _____
                                         Signature of Owner   *Date*

THE OCCUPANCY AGREEMENT AND OPTION TO PURCHASE

The occupancy agreement and the option to purchase are two contracts, but can be combined into one agreement, the option to purchase coming at the end of the occupancy agreement. An occupancy agreement can also include a utilities agreement, which names the tenants as responsible for the utilities at the property. The occupancy differs from the lease agreement because where the lease agreement is to prove to a lender you will have tenants and monthly cash flow, the occupancy agreement is more in depth and outlines the responsibilities of the tenant, specifically. The occupancy agreement is the contract between you and the tenants.

The option to purchase, often found at the end of the occupancy agreement, outlines the amount of the monthly option credits the tenant will earn as they rent the property. It also outlines the final purchase price of the property, the amount the tenant will pay for the home at the end of the rental term. The exercise of option fee is an amount of money the tenant will pay at the end of the rental term that will cover the closing costs for the sale of the home from you, the investor, to the tenants. The amount of the exercise of option fee depends on the purchase price, as well as other considerations. Speak with your mortgage broker or real estate lawyer to determine the proper amount for the exercise of option fee. What follows is a sample of an occupancy agreement, utilities agreement and option to purchase I have used in the past.

Occupancy Agreement
(Address of Property)

Received from _____ (tenants' names), hereinafter referred to as the "Occupant," the sum of $ (CDN) Dollars which upon acceptance of this agreement by _____ (your name as the investor), the owners of the premises, hereinafter referred to as the "Owner," enacted upon the date as signed below shall be applied as follows:

In the event that this agreement is not accepted by the Owner or his authorized agent, within five (5) business days, the total deposit received shall be refunded.

Occupant hereby offers to occupy the premises from the Owner, the property known as:

_____ (address, city and province) upon the following TERMS and CONDITIONS:

This agreement is subject to the Occupant obtaining a home inspection, at the Occupant's expense, within (5) business days of acceptance of the purchase and sale agreement and the report being acceptable to the Occupant and Owner. The Occupant shall have (5) five business days to give written notice to the Owner of an unacceptable Inspection report, at which time this agreement shall become null and void and all deposits are to be returned to the Occupant without deduction or delay.

Payable prior to Occupancy

Monthly Occupant Fee for the period _____ (lease commencement date), through _____(one month following the lease commencement date) $ _____ (first month lease payment)

Initial Option Payment Credit (Non-refundable) $_____   (the tenants' deposit

TOTAL DUE on _____ (lease commencement date) $_____ (the first month lease payment plus the tenants' deposit, including any monies they have paid thus far)

TERM: The term hereof shall commence on _____ (lease commencement date) and continue for a period of _____ (rental term length, in months) months, ending _____ (lease completion date).

OCCUPANCY AGREEMENT: A total monthly payment of _____ (monthly lease payment amount, written in words) Dollars (CDN) (_____) (monthly lease payment amount in numbers) consisting of an "Occupancy" payment in the amount of _____ (monthly lease payment amount minus monthly option credit, written in words) (CDN) (_____) (monthly lease payment amount minus monthly option credit, written in numbers, plus a "Monthly Option Money Payment" in the amount of _____ (monthly option credit amount, written in words) (CDN) (_____) (monthly option credit amount, written in numbers) as noted above, payable in advance, before the first day of each calendar month to the Owner at the address below, or such other place as may be designated by the Owner from time to time. In the event the payment is not received, Occupant is in Default under the agreement and is subject to the DEFAULT provisions below.

UTILITIES: The Occupant shall pay all utilities and services for the Premises (e.g., condo fees, electricity, water, sewer service, garbage collection, telephone, cable TV, and Internet) in a timely manner.
The Occupant agrees to have the electricity, natural gas, and water utilities put in his/her name as of the commencement of this Agreement. (_____) (lease commencement date)
Upon request by the Owner/Approved Agent, the Occupant shall provide proof of timely payment of such utilities and services.

USE & OCCUPANTS: The Premises shall be used as residence with no more than ____ adults and _____ children. The Premises shall not be used for any other purpose without the prior written consent of the Owner.

ASSIGNMENT & SUBLETTING: The Occupant shall not assign this Agreement or sublet the Premises or any portion thereof without the prior written consent of the Owner.

MAINTENANCE, REPAIRS AND ALTERATIONS: The Occupant acknowledges that the Premises are in good order and repair, unless otherwise indicated herein.
The Occupant shall be responsible for all repairs, maintenance costs, and service charges.

The Occupant shall water and maintain any surrounding grounds, including lawns and shrubbery, and keep the same clear of rubbish and weeds when such grounds are part of the Premises and are for the exclusive use of the Occupant.

The Occupant shall, at his own expense, maintain the Premises in a clean and sanitary manner including all equipment, appliances, furniture and furnishings therein and shall surrender the Premises at termination hereof, in good condition as received, except for normal wear and tear.

The Occupant may paint, install wallpaper or otherwise redecorate or make alterations to the Premises WITH the prior written consent of the Owner.

All costs for any redecorating or alterations shall be paid 100% by the Occupant. Should the Occupant leave or not exercise the option, or this agreement is cancelled for any reason, there will be no credit or consideration returned for repairs, alterations, or decorations.

POSSESSION: If the Owner is unable to deliver possession of the Premises at the commencement hereof, Owner shall not be liable for any damage caused thereby, nor shall this agreement be voided or voidable but Occupant shall not be liable for any monthly payments until possession is delivered.

ENTRY & INSPECTION: The Occupant shall permit the Owner or the Owner's agent to enter the Premises at reasonable times and upon reasonable notice for the purpose of inspecting the Premises or showing the same to prospective Occupants or Purchasers, or for making necessary repairs.

INSURANCE: The Occupant must maintain an owner-approved "Occupant Contents Insurance" policy and provide ongoing verification of such insurance policy to the Owner.

INDEMNIFICATION: The Owner shall not be liable for any damage or injury to the Occupant, or any other person, or to any property, occurring on the Premises, or any part thereof, or in common areas thereof, and the Occupant agrees to hold the Owner harmless from any claims for damages no matter how caused.

DEFAULT: Failure by the Occupant to pay the Monthly Occupancy fee when due, or perform any term hereof, shall, at the option of the Owner/Approved Agent, terminate all rights of Occupant hereunder. In the event that Occupant shall be absent from the premises for a period of five (5) consecutive days, while in Default, Occupant shall, at the option of the Owner, be deemed to have abandoned the premises and any property left on the premises shall be considered abandoned and may be disposed of by the owner in any manner allowed by law. In the event that the Owner reasonably believes that such abandoned property has no value, it may be discarded. The Option is immediately Null and Void and the Monthly Credits accumulated are forfeited as liquidated damages and not as a penalty. All property on the premises is hereby subject to a lien in favor of Owner, for payment of all sums due hereunder, to the maximum allowed by law;

Recover of premises by Owner shall not relieve Occupant for any obligation hereunder, and Owner may allow another Occupant in the premises upon such terms and conditions he deems proper, and recover from Occupant sums due hereunder, less any consideration received from others for the use of the premises, for the remaining term thereof, after paying expenses.

SECURITY & DEPOSIT FUNDS: The security deposit set forth above, if any, shall secure the performance of Occupant's obligations hereunder. Owner may, but shall not be obligated to apply all or portions of said deposit on account of Occupant's obligations hereunder. Any balance remaining shall be returned to the Occupant. Any returnable deposits shall be refunded within ten (10) days from date possession is delivered to Owner or his/her authorized agent.

LEGAL FEES: In the event that the Owner shall prevail in any legal action brought by either party to enforce the terms hereof or relating to the demised Premises, the Owner shall be entitled to all costs incurred in connection with such action, including legal fees of a solicitor and his own client, on a full indemnity basis. The Owner is entitled to recover an allowance for his time and effort expended with respect to any default recovery proceedings at the rate of $50.00 per hour. Such allowance is deemed to be reasonable and comparable with what the Owner would pay to a third party for a similar time and effort.

WAIVERS: No failure of the Owner to enforce any term hereof shall be deemed a waiver, nor shall any acceptance of partial payment of monthly occupancy payment be deemed a waiver of Owner's right to full amount of refund;

NOTICES: Any notice which either party may or is required to give, may be given by mailing the same, postage prepaid, to the Occupant at the Premises or to the Owner at the address shown below or at such other places as may be designated by the parties from time to time;

HEIRS, ASSIGNS, & SUCCESSORS: This Occupancy Agreement is binding upon and inures to the benefit of the heirs, assigns and successors in interest to the parties;

TIME: Time is of the essence in this Agreement.

UTILITIES AGREEMENT

This Agreement is to outline responsibilities for all utilities at the following property:

(Address of property)

The Occupant agrees to have the Hydro & Gas Utilities and water put in his/her name for the above mentioned property for the duration of this Occupancy Agreement.

Hydro
Gas

This agreement is made between,

_____ (your name, as the investor)
As the **OWNER**
AND
_____ (the tenants' names)
As **OCCUPANTS**

Failure to provide timely payments to the appropriate utility vendor is to be treated as an outstanding arrears amount that can be recoverable by the Owner just as if it were Occupancy fee owing. (This at the sole discretion of the Owner.) It is therefore agreed that default in payment may result in a breech of responsibility and enjoyment of use for fellow Occupants should payments be missed. This agreement is not intended to omit any obligations by either party to the Occupancy Agreement.

The utilities are to be paid in a timely manner as Occupant receives the bills from the providers

This agreement shall be in effect for the entire term of the Occupancy Agreement.

AGREED UPON this date:

_____

_____

Occupant: Owner:

OPTION TO PURCHASE

Initial_____ Monthly Option Payment Credit (Non-refundable) $_____ (The amount of the monthly option credit)

Estimated Total Monthly Credit at expiration of Option (___ months) $_____ (the amount of the monthly option credit, unless that amount will change, this will most likely be the same as the number above).

Initial_____ Initial Option Payment Credit (Non-refundable) $_____ (the tenant's initial deposit

TOTAL Estimated Option Payment Credit at time of purchase $_____ (the total option credit amount at the end of the rental term plus the tenants' initial deposit)

In consideration of $1.00 (ONE DOLLAR) and so long as the Occupant is not in default hereunder, Occupant shall have the option to purchase the real property described herein for a PURCHASE PRICE of $_____(CDN) (The final purchase price as determined by the appreciation rate per annum.)

EXERCISE OF OPTION: The option shall be exercised by mailing or personally delivering written notice to the Owner/Approved Agent,

60 days prior to the Expiration of Option and by additional deposit in the amount of $\underline{\$\qquad CDN}$ (the exercise of option amount, usually the same as the initial deposit amount) payable In Trust to your Solicitor.

Notice, if mailed shall be registered mail, to the Owner at the address set forth below and shall be deemed to have been given upon the day following the day shown on the post office receipt.

In the event the option is exercised, the "Original Option Money" and accumulated "Monthly Credits," if any shall be credited toward the purchase price for each month full occupancy fee has been paid when due. If the occupancy fee was late for any month, even for a period of one business day, credit will not be given for that month. These funds will only be credited if the option is exercised and the sale of the property closes. In particular, if the option is not exercised, the Occupant forfeits and the Owner retains all Options and Credits. If the option is exercised, the Security Deposit, if any, and all interest will also be credited toward the purchase price.

By exercising the option, the Occupant states that their obligation to purchase is unconditional. In particular, Occupant states that required financing (if any) is in place.

EXPIRATION OF OPTION: This option may be exercised at any time, and shall expire 45 days before the last day of the Occupancy Agreement, unless exercised prior thereto. Upon Expiration, Owner shall be released from all obligations hereunder and all Occupant's rights hereunder, legal or equitable shall cease.

THE PURCHASE

COMPLETION DATE OF PURCHASE: This date shall be 60 days from the date of exercise of the option or such other date as the parties may agree upon.

Both parties recognize that this agreement is first and foremost a residential occupancy agreement, and the Occupant must not be in default under his/her Occupant obligations in order to exercise the option.

OTHER TERMS:

WAIVER OF CONTRACTUAL RIGHT: The failure of either Party to enforce any provision of this Agreement will not be construed as a waiver or limitation of that Party's right to subsequently enforce and compel strict compliance with every provision of this Agreement;

APPLICABLE LAW: This Agreement will be construed in accordance with and governed by laws of the Province of Ontario, except as to its principles of conflicts of law;

NOTICES: Any notice which either Party may or is required to give, may be given by mailing the same postage prepaid, to Occupant at the premises or to the Owner at the address shown below or at such other places as may be designated by the Parties from time to time;

HEIRS, ASSIGNS & SUCCESSORS: This Agreement is binding upon and inures to the benefit of the heirs, assigns and successors in interest to the Parties;

TIME: Time shall be of the essence of this Agreement and of every part hereof and no extension or variation of this Agreement shall operate as a waiver of this provision;

SEVERABILITY: If any section or any portion of this Agreement is determined to be unenforceable or invalid for any reason whatsoever that the unenforceability or invalidity shall not affect the enforceability or validity of the remaining portions of this Agreement and such unenforceable and invalid section or portion thereof shall be severed from the remainder of this Agreement;

GENDER: All references to Occupant herein employed shall be construed to include the plural as well as the singular, and the masculine shall include the feminine and neuter where the context of this Agreement may require;

ENTIRE AGREEMENT: This Agreement, including and schedules attached hereto, constitutes the entire agreement between the Parties pertaining to the subject matter of this Agreement and supersedes all prior agreements, understandings, negotiations and discussions, whether written or oral, between the Parties in connection with the subject matter of this Agreement except as specifically set out in this Agreement;

EXTENSION OF AGREEMENT: If financing cannot be obtained due to no fault of the Occupant/Buyers, and provided this Agreement is in good standing and not in default, then this Agreement shall continue on a Month-to-Month basis for an additional six (6) months with no increase in the Monthly Fee or change in the Monthly Credits. The Purchase Price shall however increase at the rate of .5% per month. If after these additional (6) six months, the property still has not closed, then the Monthly Fee and Credits can, at the option and absolute full discretion of the Owner, be increased. The Purchase Price shall continue to increase at the rate of .5% per month.

LEGAL AGREEMENT: OWNER HEREBY ADVISES OCCUPANT THAT BY SIGNING THIS RESIDENTIAL OCCUPANCY AGREEMENT WITH OPTION TO PURCHASE, YOU WILL BE ENTERING INTO A LEGALLY BINDING AGREEMENT WITH OWNER. OWNER RECOMMENDS AND ADVISES THE OCCUPANT TO OBTAIN INDEPENDENT LEGAL ADVICE REGARDING THE TERMS OF THIS AGREEMENT PRIOR TO SIGNING THIS AGREEMENT. YOU ACKNOWLEDGE AND AGREE THAT YOU HAVE BEEN GIVEN SUFFICIENT OPPORTUNITY TO OBTAIN

INDEPENDENT LEGAL ADVICE. YOU FURTHER AC-
KNOWLEDGE AND AGREE THAT YOU HAVE OBTAINED
SUCH INDEPENDENT LEGAL ADVICE AS YOU CONSIDER
NECESSARY AND ADVISABLE;

**ACCEPTANCE: The undersigned Owner accepts the foregoing
and acknowledges receipt hereof. The undersigned Occupant
hereby acknowledges receipt of a copy hereof.**

IN WITNESS WHEREOF, the Parties have executed this Agreement as of:

OWNER   **OCCUPANT**

Signature: _____   Signature: _____

Printed Name: Printed Name:

OWNER   **OCCUPANT**

Signature: _____   Signature: _____

Printed Name: Printed Name:

Address for service:

_____ (address of the property)

The Home Repair Contact

In regards to the property located at _____
(Address of property) herein referred to as "the property,"
_____ (tenants, names), herein re-
ferred to as "the tenant" agree to maintain and upkeep the property
and its surrounding grounds, and agree to make any and all repairs
outlined in the house inspection within the time frame specified in the
home inspection. Failure to make these repairs will result in the loss of
deposit and option credits in order to cover the costs associated with
said repairs. Repairs are as follows:

1.   _____(repair)

     _____(date by which the issue must be resolved)

2.   _____(repair)

     _____(date by which the issue must be resolved)

3.   _____(repair)

     _____(date by which the issue must be resolved)

_____ Tenant Signature
_____ Tenant Signature
_____ Date
_____ Date

Take the initiative to go through all of the contracts with the tenant and ensure they understand all parts of the agreements. Answer any questions they
may have. Occasionally, your tenants will wish to run the contracts past their
lawyer. Do not discourage this; just as we as investors must watch out for our
own interests, the tenants also have the right to get independent legal advice.
If you have done your due diligence with the contracts you have decided to use
and run them past your own lawyer, the tenants seeking legal advice shouldn't
cause you any stress because you know your documents are sound.

Once the financing conditions have been met and any other conditions
outlined on the agreement of purchase and sale have been satisfied, the deal is
almost complete—at least this part of the deal.

TENANT INSURANCE

Before the tenant moves in, request to see a copy of their tenant insurance. This will not only cover the tenant, it will also cover you, since with their own renter's insurance, the amount of insurance you need to have is limited. Don't just take their word for it—ask to see it and take a photocopy for your files.

THE WALK-THROUGH

Before the tenant moves in, make sure you go through the house with them and discuss any repairs that need to be made, as documented in the home inspection. Take pictures of the inside and outside of the house before you hand over the keys. Once this is finished, so are you! Your tenant can now move in and their rental term begins!

THE RENTAL TERM

During the rental term, your involvement will be minimal, but that doesn't mean you get to go on sabbatical for two or three years. The rental term is a time for you to keep in contact with the tenant. Firstly, you want to make sure they are improving their credit. Sit down with them and examine their credit report to get an idea of the corrective steps they're taking, as well as other measures they may need in the future. If you wait until the rental term is up to go over their credit report, you have waited too long. If there are issues on the bureau, you no longer have time to help the tenant fix them, and you may end up having to extend the term or, depending on the severity of the issue, the client may not be able to exercise the option to purchase. That's why your involvement throughout the entire process is imperative. I recommend going over the tenant's bureaus every few months, but no less than once every three months. If the client is using a third-party credit repair program, ask to be included on their next phone call with their representative.

Also, make your presence known during the rental term. This does not have to be an "inspection" type scenario, and should never be a negative experience for the tenant. Take over a bottle of wine to congratulate them on the house. If the house inspection brought up any issues, follow up to make sure the tenants have had the problems fixed, or will be doing it shortly. Being proactive during the rental term and taking the initiative to make sure any house issues get fixed will only serve you, and will prevent a problem from magnifying.

With all of the paperwork signed, our hypothetical investor Tim is ready to become a landlord and spend the duration of the rental term making sure repairs are made to the houses, that his tenants are, in fact, taking steps to improve their credit and popping by to touch base with Gary and Rita and Jonathan and Cindy on a human level. To his surprise, he is even invited to Gary's 50th birthday party, and takes the opportunity to visit his investment property and see how the couple is doing.

IN REVIEW

Submit an offer to purchase for the tenant's choice house. Bring your mortgage broker on board to obtain financing for the property. The paperwork required to complete a tenant-first rent to own includes the intent to occupy, the lease agreement, occupancy agreement, option to purchase, utilities agreement, agreement of repairs (or home repair contract) and the offer to purchase. Ensure the tenant has proper tenant/contents insurance, and perform a walk-through with the tenants before they receive the keys, making sure to take pictures of the inside and out. During the rental term, you, the investor, must remain active with the tenants by reviewing their credit reports at least every three months and making sure they are completing any necessary repairs.

CHAPTER 15

The Deal Closes

It wouldn't be fair to leave you hanging for the duration of Jonathan and Cindy and Gary and Rita's rental terms, so let's fast-forward three years and look at the process of the house sale from you, the investor, to the tenant.

Two months (or 60 days) before the rental term comes to a close, the client can exercise the option to purchase. As outlined in the contract, they have to notify you of their intent to purchase the house, but your diligence will pay off here if you contact them two months before the end of the rental term.

THE EXERCISE OF OPTION

If you read the option to purchase contract, you may have spotted something called the "exercise of option" clause, in which there is a spot for a dollar amount. That dollar amount is the monies needed by the tenant to close the deal, or closing costs. This amount could be anywhere between $5,000 and $10,000 depending on where you live and the purchase price of the property. If you're unsure how much money should be entered on this line, this is the perfect time to open your networking file and contact your mortgage broker. He or she will be able to instruct you the amount the tenant will need to pay to close the deal.

The tenant will not pay this money to you, but instead will put it in trust with their lawyer for the costs of purchasing the property.

At that point, you will have an offer to purchase drawn up. Naturally, since you have a pre-negotiated purchase price, there will be no thrilling negotiations like when we first purchased the property (whew!). Once the offer to purchase is ready and signed by all parties, the tenant will use their mortgage broker to obtain financing and get the commitment from a lender.

A major difference between the initial purchase of the property and the sale to the tenant is the lack of a realtor. Make sure that the tenant has a good mortgage broker, though. If they don't, why not set them up with one? It's in everyone's best interests for your tenant to get a great mortgage that suits their needs.

After that, all that's left is the waiting. The deal will soon close, you will sell the property and you can move on to your next tenant-first rent-to-own deal.

CHAPTER 16

Tenant FAQs

As you progress with tenant-first rent to own, you will notice the same questions coming from potential tenants. Eventually, answering these questions will become second nature, but as you are starting out, it's a good idea to have answers in an easily accessible place for quick reference. Below is a list of the most common tenant Q&A scenarios.

If you are creating a website, include an area where you can send tenants to get more information. This will significantly reduce the amount of time you spend answering common questions with applicants. If you're not starting a website, you can also prepare an information sheet to give to applicants when you meet with them. These tools will help you leverage your time, freeing you up to do the things you need to do to close deals.

WHY DO I HAVE TO SEND MONEY UPFRONT?

The initial amount they send to get the ball rolling (I recommend $500 but you can set this amount however you like) is a show of good faith on the tenants' part. You will be spending your time and money to review applicants, do your due diligence, set them up with a realtor and more. The initial payment demonstrates they're serious and want to move forward. This amount comes out of their total deposit, so if their deposit is $7,000 and they send $500 up front, they will need to give you an additional $6,500, and all of that goes toward their down payment at the end of the rental term. The tenant receives the intent to occupy contract, which explains in an official capacity that if the deal falls apart for any reason other than their own making, they receive their money back.

WHO WILL SEE MY PERSONAL INFORMATION?

In this day and age, with identity theft a harsh reality, people guard their personal information, such as social insurance numbers, credit reports, T4s and NOAs. Inform the applicant that the only person who will see their personal information is you (or, if you have others working with you, an administrator or joint-venture partners). When they locate a credit repair specialist, they will provide their personal information to that person, and no other people will be privy to their private information. Canadians are protected by PIPEDA, or the Personal Information Protection and Electronic Documents Act. For more information about the act and the things you must do to be in legal compliance, visit www.priv.gc.ca.

WHAT HAPPENS IF I CAN'T PURCHASE THE HOUSE AT THE END OF THE RENTAL TERM?

This is a common concern, especially in a weak economy. I inform tenants that the situation would have to be addressed at the time, depending on the reasons they are unable to purchase the house. If they stick to their credit repair plan, they should have no problem qualifying at the end of the rental term. If the reason is due to job loss or going on a last-minute spending spree, the situation would need to be discussed further. Tell the tenant because you are a private investor and not a traditional lender such as a bank, you address issues on a case-by-case basis, and do not have a standard clause that applies to every situation. Reassure them, however, that as long as they genuinely are making strides in repairing their credit or saving their down payment, there are things that can be done, such as a rental term extension. It is also important to mention that in this case, if they simply change their mind, they will forfeit their initial deposit as well as any option credits they have earned throughout the rental period.

HOW MUCH OF A DEPOSIT DO I NEED TO PUT DOWN?

The deposit required is between 2 and 5% of the purchase price of the home. The larger deposit a tenant can put down, the better it will be for them because the deposit is credited toward the purchase price at the end of the rental term. Also, the bigger the deposit, the more flexibility you can provide when determining the tenant's monthly lease payments.

WHO IS IN CHARGE OF MAINTENANCE?

The tenant is responsible for all maintenance and repairs to the property, including any initial issues that may be discovered during the home inspection.

WHO PAYS FOR THE HOME INSPECTION?

The tenant is responsible for the cost of the home inspection, and their involvement in the actual inspection is mandatory. Since the house will be theirs, they need to know ahead of time any issues with the house and the actions they will need to take, both immediately and in the future, to ensure the house continues to be in a state of good repair.

WHO PAYS FOR THE PROPERTY TAXES?

During the rental term, you, the investor, pay the property taxes. After the tenant exercises the option to purchase, they will then be responsible for the taxes.

WHAT ABOUT INSURANCE?

You, the investor, will be responsible for property insurance during the rental term, after which the tenant must take out their own property insurance. During the rental term, the tenant must have renters/contents insurance, and you must verify this as part of your due diligence.

WHO PAYS FOR UTILITIES?

Just like a rental scenario, the tenant is responsible for the utilities including water, heat, gas, hydro and any other utilities payments that may apply, depending on the province they will be living in.

# CHAPTER 17

Worst-Case Scenario

Now let's take a look at the risks of a tenant-first rent to own, in a section I like to call "Worst-Case Scenario." The fact that this strategy seems "too good to be true" is both a good and bad thing. It's good because we're looking at a strong investment strategy with low to zero risk that yields a huge return in a short period of time, usually only a few years. It can be bad, though, because many investors will look at the opportunity and think there is something they're missing, a large grey area into which their life savings could disappear.

When beginning any type of investment, everyone plays the worst-case scenario game to some extent, imagining all of the things that could go wrong and how they could be handled before they even occur. In the spirit of sceptical investors everywhere, let's outline some of the things that could potentially go wrong, regardless of how extreme or unlikely they seem, to put your mind at ease as much as possible so you can see the true potential of this investment strategy.

Fortunately, with this tenant-first rent-to-own strategy, there is nothing we will talk about that cannot ultimately become beneficial for you, the investor, in the long run. The "worst-case scenario" situations we're about to discuss are real questions investors starting out with tenant-first rent to own have asked me, so hopefully we will cover enough to set your mind at ease.

Worst-case scenario 1: What if the tenant pulls a midnight move?

The chances of your tenant moving out in the middle of the night are low. Why? Because we have their deposit, of course! Not to mention a legal document they have signed stating they will not receive that money back in any other form than toward their down payment, and only at the end of the rental term, when they exercise their option to purchase the house. They also forfeit all option credits they have accumulated up until that point. That is a lot of money from which to walk away, but, in a heightened circumstance in which they do pull a runner by the light of the moon, you pocket the deposit and option credits accumulated and begin advertising for another tenant. The process begins again as a traditional rent-to-own investment, but you obtain a new deposit from your new tenants. You have quite the chunk of money for your "inconvenience," which really would be a blessing in disguise; it's better to know early that the tenant is not serious than at the end of the term. Use the deposit to cover the mortgage for a month until you can replace them with a new rent-to-own tenant. Failing that, you can always rent the property out as a traditional rental. It would be inconvenient and take a lot of your time and energy if a tenant moves out on you in the night, but financially, you can quickly get the investment up and running once again.

In all of the time I have been involved with rent to own, I have never experienced a midnight move. So, put your mind at ease, as this is a heightened circumstance if one ever existed.

Worst-case scenario 2: What if the tenants trash the house?

This is a very common concern for investors: how do I know my investment is protected? In the case of rent to own in general, and this tenant-first strategy in particular, this is a very rare circumstance, indeed. The tenant is clearly serious about home ownership, or they would not have come up with the cash for the deposit. They have also spent a lot of time with the realtor choosing the perfect house, one they love. Even though the house is not yet theirs on paper, for all intents and purposes, in the tenants' mind, they own the home. But, if this did happen, firstly you have a contract drawn up stating the tenants are responsible for all repairs and maintenance. This would especially ring true of damages they have inflicted on the property. If you are a proper sceptic, your next question will be "What if they deny the damages were their fault, and simply say the house was like that when they got it?" Well, the answer to that is simple: if you remember, before the tenant moved into the house, we did a complete walk-through with them, took pictures of the property and had them sign the paperwork stating the property was in the condition stated on the form.

Throughout my many years of rent-to-own investing, never once have I witnessed a tenant trash their house.

Worst-case scenario 3: What if a tenant gets hurt on the property and claims you are liable?

Any time you are threatened with words such as "liable," seek professional legal help immediately. This would be another time you could make use of your network. Your lawyer can advise you of the best course of action. But, as with the other worst-case scenarios, this is not a common situation.

Once again, though, your initial agreements with the tenant will serve you best, as a well-crafted liability clause in the original documentation in this situation will cover your, er, assets.

Worst-case scenario 4: What if a tenant does not pay their rent?

This scenario is more likely than the others, simply because sometimes things happen that are out of the tenants' control. If it's the first time and they have a good reason, it could be just a one-off that may never happen again.

There are steps you can take to decrease the likelihood that a tenant will bounce their rent cheques. First, make sure there are provisions written into your lease agreement, allowing you to collect fees for late payment and bounced cheques, evict and, if necessary, take steps to recoup the money you are owed.

The second precaution to prevent a tenant not paying their rent is to get post-dated cheques—for the entire rental term! There is nothing worse than having to chase down a tenant for another set of rent cheques, or even worse, each month. Save yourself the time and stress and get all of their cheques ahead of time. If they change banks or bank accounts, you can always get new cheques from them later.

Third, lay out clearly defined ramifications. The tenant should know ahead of time the consequences of bouncing a cheque, and these act as a deterrent. If a tenant does bounce a cheque, make sure you follow through on these consequences, no matter how much you personally like the people. If at your first opportunity you overlook the mistake, you are indirectly telling them it is okay.

Nine times out of 10, when a landlord overlooks a bounced cheque, the tenants bounce another in the near future. Save yourself the hassle right off the bat and teach your tenants that bouncing cheques is not okay.

Consequences can be things such as charging an NSF (non-sufficient funds) or a late payment fee. More drastic consequences can even be immediate eviction. It all depends on what kind of precedent you want to set and how hard you want to be.

If the tenant does not pay at all, after a period of time you will need to look at preparing to evict. Eviction is a lengthy process in Canada, so make sure you know what the process entails in your province. Remember, if eviction is your only option, you will not be destitute. You have their original deposit, option credits, and most of the time you can fill a property rather quickly, if not with another rent-to-own tenant then with a renter—for now.

As with all other aspects of any real estate investing venture, be sure you check the landlord/tenant act in your province and know your rights, especially if you're setting up a "no strikes" system, where you will evict on the first folly. Procedures and timelines for eviction and collecting late rent vary, so invest the time to get educated on what a late or missed rent payment means for you.

In my personal experience, I have had tenants bounce rent cheques for a number of reasons, but none of them was reason enough to evict. Because I use absolute integrity when qualifying a tenant, I have never encountered a situation where they simply did not pay their rent and I had to evict.

Worst-case scenario 5: What if the tenant wants to buy out early?

As we discussed previously when we were looking at rental terms, after viewing the credit bureau, you will assess the tenant a rental term based on their credit situation. You should never give a tenant a three-year term when they can clean up their credit in just one or two years. So, if you have done your job properly, the tenant with credit issues will not be able to qualify for a mortgage before the end of the rental term. I always get this question, though, in one form or another. "But," people ask, "what if they can?" In a credit repair situation, anything short of a miracle from God would not be enough to get them a mortgage with their bad credit, but I am willing to humor them. So, I advise the tenant that in these heightened "divine intervention" type scenarios, we could discuss the possibility of them exercising the option to purchase early. This is no sweat off my back, since my exit strategy is well mapped out. Selling the house to the tenant after two years rather than three means I can turn a profit faster and set up my next investment sooner.

A tenant being able to buy out early is not so ludicrous in a situation where the tenant has good credit but just needed time to save up their deposit. It's common for a tenant to get a raise at work or a bonus, an inheritance or, heck, they could even win the lottery! Crazier things have happened in the world of rent to own, so there is a better chance of these tenants wanting to buy out early than those with bad credit.

Again, in these cases, I am willing to discuss it with the tenant. It may benefit me in the end to get out of the deal early, or it may not. If a tenant saving up for a down payment asks if they're able to exercise their option to purchase early, it's entirely up to you whether you hold them to the original rental term. But don't shut the door on the possibility, because it could, once again, be a win/win situation for everyone involved.

In my rent-to-own career, only one group of tenants was able to exercise their option to purchase early, due to a windfall that afforded them the down payment the bank required. I was more than happy to accommodate them—in fact, I was almost as happy for them as they were.

Worst-case scenario 6: What if a tenant is unable to buy the house at the end of the rental term?

This is a rare situation, because if the client has poor credit and has followed your suggestions for credit repair, this situation will probably not come about. Sometimes things happen, though, which may prevent a tenant from purchasing the house, despite their intentions. If, at the end of the rental term they're unable to purchase the house, again it's up to you what you do. If it's because they were unable to sufficiently clean up their credit, or are still short on the down payment, you have the option to extend the rental term to give them more time. If you decide not to, which you might do if the tenant has gone and applied for more credit or not stuck to their repair program, then the client loses their deposit and option credits, as per the original agreement. With the tenant out, you have the option to get another tenant in the house, either on a traditional rent-to-own or a standard rental agreement.

Worst-case scenario 7: What if the house appraises for less than the predetermined purchase price?

This is a fair question, especially in the current markets where house prices have drastically dropped over the last two years. A lot can happen within a two- to three-year rental term, and that can include a drop in property values. Of course, if your predetermined purchase price is $410,000 but the house appraises for only $390,000 at the end of the rental term, no one, I don't care who they are, will be able to get that person a mortgage for the original price. In this case, there are many options, as we want to keep the scenario a win/win. You could extend the rental term to see if the appraisal goes up as the markets change. You could also hold a second mortgage on the property for the difference if the tenants have paid on time during the whole rental period. In some situations, the tenants may want to walk away if the difference between purchase price and appraisal is too great, in which case all you would need to do is advertise for a new rent-to-own tenant.

The next question I receive after this one is "What if the house appraises for more? Do I have to pay the higher price?" The answer is no. The predetermined purchase price is, essentially, a maximum (before closing costs, of course) that the tenant will pay to purchase the house.

 **Appendix**

Checklist

Final Checklist

Getting started

- [ ] Time
- [ ] Money
- [ ] Organization
- [ ] Take care of business
- [ ] The will to succeed
- [ ] Fill out Getting Started Action Plan chart and create your plan

Build your network by meeting

- [ ] Realtors
- [ ] Mortgage brokers
- [ ] Credit repair specialists
- [ ] Real estate lawyers
- [ ] Home inspectors
- [ ] Insurance broker or agent
- [ ] Accountant/bookkeeper

Find the tenant

- [ ] Advertise for tenants
- [ ] Receive completed applications
- [ ] Narrow down the applicants
- [ ] Qualify the applicants
- [ ] Do your due diligence

❑ Run the numbers through the financial analysis spreadsheet
❑ Approve the tenant
❑ Advise tenant of lease rate, option credit and final purchase price
❑ Collect intent to occupy and initial deposit

Find the property

❑ Set up the tenant with a realtor
❑ Arrange home inspection
❑ Submit the offer to purchase
❑ Obtain financing
❑ Draft lease agreement
❑ Draft occupancy agreement
❑ Draft utilities agreement
❑ Draft option to purchase
❑ Draft the home repair contract

Arrange financing

❑ Contact your mortgage broker

The rental term

❑ Follow up with tenants every three months at the most to discuss their credit bureaus
❑ Make your presence known
❑ Ensure tenants are performing necessary repairs

The deal closes

❑ Contact tenant a few months before the rental term ends
❑ Have tenant put exercise of option fee in trust with lawyer
❑ Draw up offer to purchase

Index